Noah Dikgale

Proclaim Liberty

Acknowledgements
Front cover painting by John French
Designed by bwa

Editorial support and advice from
Roger Williamson
Editorial work by Eldred Willey and
Janet Banks
Design and publishing advice from
Bridget Middleton
Marketing advice from Sam O'Sullivan
Photographic advice from Joseph Cabon
Advice on title from Janet Morley

Woodcuts reprinted from *Passion in
Südafrica* (Frankfurt, 1979), with
permission from the editor, Hans Blum.

Proclaim Liberty

Proclaim Liberty: reflections on theology and debt

Proclaim Liberty

Foreword

As the new millennium approaches, it is clear that freedom from debt for the poorest peoples of the world has become the big idea which fires people's imagination. The celebration of the 2,000th anniversary of our Lord's birth should not just be a huge party. It should also be a time for reflection upon how such grave imbalances have developed in the world, and for action to rectify this tragic situation. It is a good moment to demand a new start for all who have been excluded from the feast of life through debt and slavery.

Situations of total dependence and enforced poverty are the opposite of growth into full humanity. Unfortunately they are not foreign to the experience of many in our world today. 1.3 billion people live on less than US $1.00 per day. Every second, one person is born into bad, unpayable debt in the world's poorest countries.

The image of slavery, which I emphasise in my contribution to this book, is indeed shocking. Some will question whether it is appropriate to the international debt crisis. If we look at the Old Testament, we see that the experiences of slavery, and liberation from slavery into the promised land, deeply marked the religious consciousness of the people of Israel.

Today we face the situation where countries are unable to maintain their health service or their primary education systems in order to service unpayable debts. Surely there must be a point beyond which it is legitimate to say, as Dario Fo, winner of the Nobel literature prize does: 'Can't pay; won't pay.'

The image of slavery is in the Christian Aid report *The New Abolitionists*. Perhaps I can suggest the following analogies between slavery and the international debt crisis:

1. At the time when slavery began to be challenged it was a highly profitable, highly organised, international business. Its advocates saw no alternative to it. Many argued that one could not run a successful economy without slave labour. Gradually slavery became challengeable;

then it became highly dubious; finally it became unacceptable. Even arguments that 'if we don't do it, somebody else will' could not stop legislation to outlaw slavery.

2. The slaves themselves opposed the system. We in the creditor nations must listen carefully to the voices of those articulating the cry of the people in the indebted nations of the South. One recalls the voice of Tanzania's former President, Julius Nyerere, 'Must we starve our children to pay our debts?' Within the Anglican Communion, a number of my fellow bishops in the indebted countries have spoken out with clarity and passion.

3. Slavery became increasingly unprofitable. The growing resistance to it and the growing awareness of alternatives meant that the system became less and less tenable. The same is true of the international debt system today. The costs, both human and financial, of enforcing repayment are becoming too high.

4. Slavery as a system ended partly because there was principled opposition in the rich nations which benefited from the system. There is a clear message here for those of us who live in the creditor nations today.

I believe that the Lambeth Conference is a unique opportunity, strategically falling just before the new millennium, for the Anglican bishops worldwide to speak out prophetically on international debt. The process has already begun and is partly documented in these pages. In December 1998 the Jubilee Assembly of the World Council of Churches will be held in Harare. The Lutheran and Reformed Churches of the world have already taken up this issue strongly. His Holiness Pope John Paul II has called, in his millennium statement, *Tertio Millennio Adveniente*, for Christians 'to raise their voice on behalf of all the poor and to make a call for reducing substantially, if not cancelling outright, the international debt which threatens the future of many nations' (para 51). The Jubilee 2000 movement, meanwhile, is gaining strength day by day on a global scale.

Governments are beginning to listen. I, along with other religious leaders in the UK, have had two very fruitful meetings with the British

Chancellor of the Exchequer, Gordon Brown. He has recognised the strong religious and moral arguments put forward concerning the need for renewed vigour in dealing with the problems of unsustainable debt in poor countries, and has praised the Churches for keeping the debt crisis on the public agenda. I am encouraged too by a new openness in the international financial institutions.

We should not be complacent or naive, however. There are hard questions to be addressed. Should debt relief be given to corrupt governments? Will the financial system be undermined if the debt is forgiven, and won't debts just accumulate once again? Should not those who have borrowed pay back what they owe? A full analysis of the international debt crisis in its various forms since 1970 gives a sad picture of human folly and worse. Governments have squandered loans on unsuitable projects and the purchase of arms. There was reckless borrowing and lending.

Perhaps there is a danger of oversimplification in the campaigning slogans which are used to raise awareness of complex economic and moral issues. Nonetheless, it must be said that the international debt crisis is a scandal. The Churches have a particular responsibility to campaign in an informed manner for economic and political strategies which reinforce the Christian message of the human dignity of all, since all are made in the image of God. The modern enslavement of debt and the Christian message that Jesus Christ has come to offer life in all its fullness (John 10:10) stand in the starkest contradiction.

The following collection of essays makes an important contribution to understanding the urgency of the debt crisis today, and to our responses to it. I commend it to you as a useful resource and a thought-provoking guide for your prayer and action.

The Archbishop of Canterbury

Proclaim Liberty

Introduction

The current debt crisis of some of the poorest countries in the world has become one of the most pressing issues of our time. It is the shadow that looms over the millennium. It is the scandal that will not go away. The debt crisis plays a major role in perpetuating the massive scale of poverty around the world, and the gross inequalities between nations, and within nations. It is also one of the most potent obstacles to a just and sustainable development, not just for the poorest nations, but for the whole world.

Resolving the debt crisis is not, of course, a panacea. On its own, it will not guarantee the elimination of poverty, nor end the needless deaths of millions of children from easily preventable diseases. But without it, there is little hope of reaching these aims. Debt relief forms an absolutely essential part of ending the terrible and shameful spectre of global want.

The enormity of the debt crisis, and the human suffering that trails in its wake, represent a real challenge to Christians today. Responding to it must be a priority for those who take seriously the Gospel message, and Jesus' proclamation that he came to preach good news to the poor (Luke 4:18). The millennium has given this challenge huge symbolic significance, as we seek to define how to celebrate the anniversary of Jesus Christ's birth. But the millennium is also a moment in which we have to decide what kind of twenty-first century we want to live in, whether it will be one of technological brilliance for the few or of a decent standard of living and justice for the many.

Debt poses a moral challenge to the Christian community, and the world as a whole, on the eve of the millennium. It is this challenge that the following collection addresses.

The collection of papers gathered in this book is primarily intended to offer a theological and economic resource for Anglican bishops attending the section on the international debt crisis at the Lambeth Conference of July 1998. For that reason, most of the contributions, with the exception of the pieces by Professor Sir Hans Singer, Dr Pat Logan and Ann Pettifor, are from an Anglican perspective, and the book is a specifically Anglican contribution to theological reflection on debt.

The collection also brings together some of the immensely powerful reflections about debt from a Christian perspective already in existence. In so doing, it aims not just to make these reflections accessible to a wider audience, but also to put them in constructive engagement with each other and to show the breadth of the theological dimension to the debt crisis.

The collection is, then, intended for a larger audience beyond the Lambeth Conference, and beyond the Anglican Communion. It is hoped that it will be of interest to people from other denominations who are concerned to respond to the challenge of debt from a faith perspective, and who might find some theological and economic pointers here with which to do so.

The debt issue is increasingly becoming an international and ecumenical one. Pope John Paul II has called for international debt to be addressed by Christians in his encyclical on the millennium, *Tertio Millennio Adveniente*. Several world confessional families have spoken out about debt, including the Lutheran World Federation, the World Alliance of Reformed Churches, the World Methodist Council and the Mennonite Central Committee. The All Africa Conference of Churches, the Latin American Conference of Churches, the Conference of European Churches and the Second European Ecumenical Assembly have all likewise made statements on debt. The World Council of Churches, meanwhile, has begun preparing for its December 1998 Assembly in Harare at which debt will be a major issue. These preparations have included a meeting specifically on faith responses to debt in Malaga, Spain, in April 1998. Margarita Banda at the WCC has also been collecting the responses of WCC member churches to the debt issue.

The combined voices of Churches and aid agencies calling for debt cancellation are beginning to be heard. Just before this book went to press, the director of the World Bank, James Wolfensohn, stated that present efforts to secure debt relief for the poorest countries would be pushed forward, and that some 15-16 countries will qualify for relief by 2000.[1] Much remains to be done, however. As Professor Hans Singer makes clear in his contribution to this book, the present debt relief Initiative (the Heavily Indebted Poor Countries (HIPC) Initiative) has serious flaws which need to be addressed in order for debt relief to be effective and to offer the poor of the world a real source of hope for the future.

This collection has a definite geographic bias towards Africa. This reflects the fact that the largest and growing proportion of Anglican church members are now in Africa. It also reflects the geographic location of debt: of the 41 most Heavily Indebted Poor Countries, 32 are in Africa. There is, finally, a theological rationale for focusing on Africa. As William Temple said of Simon of Cyrene, the one African in the gospels, 'How true it is that Africa has been compelled to carry the burden of a whole world's sin.' [2]

Ultimately, this collection is a call for people to act upon their faith, and to get involved in the growing movement seeking to bring about the cancellation of debt. By so doing, they will play their part in proclaiming liberty to the oppressed.

Susan Hawley
Christian Aid, 1 May 1998

1   *The Guardian*, April 15, 1998 p 3.
2   William Temple, *Readings in St John's Gospel: first and second series*, London and Basingstoke: Macmillan Press, 1970.

Let me begin by stating that if there are any who question why we bishops and archbishops, as religious leaders, should have the temerity to discuss and pronounce upon the topic of debt, and to engage the secular world on it, my response is thus: we should resist the cry that Christian leaders should keep out of politics on the grounds that the founder of Christianity did not! Our faith, in common with most of the world's religions, relates to the whole of life. We do not switch our faith on and off like an electric light bulb as we move in and out of different aspects of life.

Chains around Africa may seem an exaggerated description of this great continent. Surely, many will say, the twentieth century has been a century of astonishing progress in which Africa has shared. Of the issues at the top of the agenda as the century began, slavery has gone, colonialism and the overt suppression of black people by their white masters have all but disappeared. Since then, we have witnessed not only huge leaps in political and educational emancipation but also the supposedly unlimited opportunities offered by globalisation. And, furthermore, some will say, look at South Africa. If you are looking for a sign of hope in these times, the dismantling of apartheid is surely one. It may seem then that the description 'Chains around Africa' belongs to the world of hyperbole and does not accord with reason and reality. So what is this crisis of which I speak?

The crisis

Listen to the words of a Christian Aid document called *The New Abolitionists*:

> *More children could die unnecessary deaths before the year 2000 as a result of the debt crisis that enslaves poor countries today than were killed in passage during the infamous Atlantic slave trade. For every second that passes, another child is born into unpayable debt in the world's poorest countries. From Mozambique to Tanzania … more is spent on servicing external debt than on either education or health.*

Proclaim Liberty

The same document goes on to state that in the course of the Atlantic trade an estimated 24 million people were enslaved. In 1997, the United Nations Development Programme estimated that 21 million children would die before 2000 unless the debt crisis is resolved.

Africa is not alone in this of course. But, of the 20 most heavily indebted poor countries, as defined by the World Bank, 16 are in Africa. The external debt of those 16 countries amounts to very nearly $100 billion. If you add in the figures for other countries, the total debt for sub-Saharan Africa is $235 billion. That is the size of the problem. The extent to which these chains of indebtedness are contributing to the overall problems of Africa and the sufferings of her people simply cannot be overestimated. In Britain, every two years we have a special appeal called Comic Relief. The last appeal raised an amazing £26 million; but £22 million per day is being drained from Africa in servicing its debt.

At the Commonwealth Heads of Government meeting in Edinburgh in October 1997 the Economic Declaration recognised this:

We believe that world peace, security and social stability cannot be achieved in conditions of deep poverty and growing inequality.

And the Heads of Government agreed:

to work towards a comprehensive solution of the debt problem, and pursue vigorously the rapid implementation of the Heavily Indebted Poor Countries (HIPC) Initiative, in line with the Mauritius Mandate.

The Mauritius Mandate of September 1997, in turn, seeks to ensure that substantial progress has been made by the year 2000 in enabling all eligible poor countries to reduce their debt to sustainable levels. This is undoubtedly progress, and I am glad to be able to acknowledge the leading role that the British Government is taking in these initiatives. I was present myself at a meeting just before Christmas 1997, called by the Chancellor of the Exchequer and the Secretary of State for International Development, in which they both pledged again their support for the task, and their willingness to listen to and work alongside faith communities and non-governmental organisations (NGOs) in their campaigns. (It was heart-warming to find representatives of all the main Churches and other faiths present, and of one mind on this issue.)

Recognition of the significance of the debt problem is, of course, not new. Already in 1986 the Justice and Peace Commission at the Vatican called attention to the problem. Two years later, the Lambeth Conference of Anglican bishops added its voice with a clear message:

> *Crippling levels of debt which add intolerable burdens to the poorer nations of our world raise sharp moral questions. Debt of this nature creates unhealthy dependencies of the weak upon the powerful, leads to the breakdown of the life of poor communities and threatens the relationships of international politics and finance.*

In 1990, at the opening of the Commonwealth Finance Ministers meeting, which led to the adoption of the Trinidad proposals, the Commonwealth Secretary-General noted that:

> *net resources in excess of $40 billion have in the past year flowed from the poor developing countries to the rich industrial countries of the North, and, in addition, developing countries faced increasing obstacles to many of their exports.*

The trend continues to this day, and even the World Bank recognises it as a problem. The President of the Bank has made clear his desire to find a resolution, and as early as 1994, in the Bank's report *Adjustment in Africa*, it was noted that the Trinidad arrangement, and the earlier Toronto terms, did not do enough. Under the Trinidad terms, only six of the sub-Saharan African countries would be assisted towards a sustainable debt burden, whilst nine would still have a ratio in excess of 300% of exports.

In addressing this situation, it is important for us not to create enemies. There is a determination in the air to find a resolution, and we need to work in partnership with one another if a lasting solution is to be found. Of course, we all come at it from different perspectives. The World

Bank and other financial institutions have naturally tended to see it as primarily an economic problem, and the structural adjustment programmes that have been implemented in various countries are aimed at creating more stable and productive economic conditions. They have not always had equal regard for the social consequences of their programmes, although I believe attitudes in the World Bank are changing.

Churches and other agencies working with and amongst the poorest people in the continent are likely to come from the opposite direction. Our observation is that the poor are getting poorer. And the evidence and the testimony of the Churches and other faith communities should be taken seriously, as we are there with our people.

Debtor governments, of course, are caught in between. They realise that they have a financial duty to respond to the demands of their creditors. They have no choice. Such is the power of the international community (represented by the World Bank and the IMF) that they must comply with the conditions imposed. If they do not, growth and progress are impossible. If they do, the burden is transferred to the very poor who are crushed by the extra demands, and at a stroke isolated from a world community which is getting steadily richer as every year goes by. The irony is, as the Christian Aid publication puts it:

Where slaves were once sent with a price attached to them, now children are born with a debt around their necks. In Tanzania each new baby owes in the region of $250; in Mozambique, $350.

What is clear, however, is that we all – governments of both creditor and debtor nations, international financial institutions, Churches, people of all faiths, and NGOs – need to work together to confront the crisis directly and urgently so that the millennium can truly be seen to be a time of new beginnings for this great continent of Africa.

Crisis and *kairos*

There is a temptation today to use dramatic language rather too freely. Everything is portrayed, as it were, in banner headlines, and keywords like disaster and crisis are employed at every opportunity to catch people's attention. But what happens when a crisis persists? The media attention span is extraordinarily short, and the general level of interest amongst the public difficult to sustain. The crisis which Africa faces has been in the making for very many years, and African peoples have been seeking to resolve the problems themselves, often quite alone. One of the most desolate cries I have heard on my visits is, 'We are forgotten'. I understand why people feel that way. They are noticed internationally – or so it seems – only when disaster strikes or when some event occurs which directly affects us in the West. As one recent commentator has noted:

The beauty, tenacity and hopefulness in the vast majority of African communities is never conveyed, nor are their own efforts to transform the economic and political structures that perpetuate the inequalities which sustain chronic hunger.

That is very important. It is easy to assume that if there is to be a solution to the problems, it will eventually come at some moment when creditor institutions finally agree decisively to forgive debt. So, we look to the future, we wait, we hope, and we look to others. And the crisis continues.

But there is an alternative way of looking at things, a way based upon the concept of time in biblical theology, which, I believe, may help us all to work more constructively together to address Africa's crisis.

The New Testament has two words for time: *chronos*, from which our word chronology comes, refers to ordinary time, marked by our watches and clocks and calendars. But there is another word for time which refers to the significance of a moment in time – in the same way that a particular date is significant to us because of its association with an anniversary, such as a wedding, or the award of a degree, or the loss of a dear friend. This word, *kairos*, speaks profoundly of hope, of God breaking into ordinary time and filling it with his presence. It is a jubilee moment in which a new start is made.

I believe we have arrived at a decisive moment for Africa. We must not allow it to pass, nor to threaten us in any way. Rather, it is the moment of opportunity. It is, as the Roman Catholic Archbishop of Tabora wrote recently:

A Kairos, a very positive moment, a moment for critically and deeply evaluating the present situation and the past decades.

I would simply want to go one step further to say that it is the moment also for concerted action.

Responsibility for action

Churches and faith communities have a heavy responsibility. We must recognise that in some parts of Africa we contribute to the problems rather than the solutions. All people of faith should be collaborating in common action to alleviate suffering, and rejecting the sort of rivalry which has led from time to time to violent confrontation. Africa cannot afford such competition, and no authentic religious teaching condones such behaviour.

We, probably more than any other organisation, are in touch with the people. We must enable their voice to be heard. We must tell the story that the suffering of the people of Africa is immense. We must work together to ensure that the moment is not lost, and that the moment of crisis is seized as a moment of opportunity rather than ignored as a prelude to disaster. We need to ensure that this message is conveyed to the world. The facts must be shared with ordinary citizens of the First World who are largely ignorant of the real situation Africa faces. But I want to say to my fellow faith leaders, to theologians, to all people of faith, that addressing this *kairos* moment is our key task. We must see in the crisis the hope which will set God's people free.

One well-known African theologian has written recently:

Nothing can blind us to this brutal fact: Africa today is crucified. An African theology that re-reads the Bible in terms of the fundamental locus will have to be a theology of the Cross.

That sober assessment is correct. Yet, any theology of the cross must always take into account the resurrection as well, for that is the completion of the story. Out of death comes new life, out of hopeless situations come opportunities; from crisis comes hope. That is the message we must continue to press, for the temptation is always to lose hope.

It was the Nigerian statesman, Olusegun Obasanjo, who wrote:

Throughout history, many people have found their feet when and where they were about to be written off, and have been able to be active and important members of the world. I believe that will be the situation in Africa.

He went on to say:

If we work with the international community on the basis of partnership in the economic area, in conflict management, and in promoting democracy, we stand a better chance of making it.

Now, I am sure that everyone accepts that responsibilities also lie with governments in Africa. I have to say that I meet indignation among investment bankers in London or New York whenever the issue of international debt is raised. It is pointed out very forcefully that the obligation to combat corruption must be a *sine qua non* of debt cancellation. There is scarcely any point in waiving debt if the resulting gains are simply diverted into the pockets of corrupt leaders and officials who are unaccountable to the people.

I agree with that and believe that the Churches and all faith groups have a role to play in nurturing societies all over the world where justice and moral responsibility replace corruption and greed. Of course, we in the West must fight shy of being over-prescriptive in our attempts to support development in Africa. Africa must be free to develop in its own way. But there are certain fundamental concepts which we would all hope to see honoured, which will create confidence in the partnership. We look for transparency and accountability in government, justice and care for the weakest members of society, appropriate forms of democracy, ethical trading, proper working conditions for workers, and recognition of basic human rights, matched by co-responsibility to others.

Yet, while it is entirely proper to remind Africa of her moral responsibilities, we from Europe and elsewhere must recall that we have moral responsibilities too, because of the colonial legacy. The structures which many countries inherited on independence have not been easy to work with. The national boundaries which the colonial powers drew up, and their preoccupation with nation-building, paid scant attention to the ethnic arrangements and traditional structures of African life. 'Divide and Rule' was the familiar strategy of Empire and it created problems which had not previously existed.

So we have heavy responsibilities too. We are not just interested and concerned onlookers. We in the West are intimately involved in Africa, and not just historically. Indeed, we have a moral responsibility to find ways of reducing substantially the crushing burden of debt which compromises the economies of entire nations and sends millions to early graves. I applaud the progress which has been made in recent times, but urge the rich governments of the world to meet the moral challenge.

Over the past few years, the Churches have been pushing for the biblical concept of jubilee to be accepted to mark the millennium. The year 2000 is such a symbolic moment, truly a *kairos* moment. Christian countries influenced so profoundly by the coming of Christ 2000 years ago will, if we are not careful, treat the anniversary as a mere moment of time. We can do so much more than simply celebrate a date. It will become a *kairos* moment if we have the moral courage to take the chains off Africa by relieving her of the burden of unpayable debt.

At the heart of our Christian faith stands a prayer taught by Jesus, the sentiments of which are surely universal. In one form of that prayer we pray:
Forgive us our debts, as we forgive those who are our debtors.
We are all in some way in debt to one another. We have throughout history trespassed against one another, and in the context of the future development of Africa, the legacy is one of suppressed potential and heavy

burdens. Africa is in chains. We have the opportunity to forgive one another in very practical ways, to ensure that those chains are finally broken.

As I look around Africa, I see a continent which is bursting with potential. The opportunities are boundless. Now is the time for us all to repent of those things which have created this crisis which has led to Africa's captivity. This year marks the 50th anniversary of the UN Declaration of Human Rights. The lives of millions of Africans fall far short of the ideals set out in that historic document. Let us re-commit ourselves to those ideals. The millennium is a symbolic opportunity to transform crisis into hope. Let us grasp it together, with common purpose. As one of my Sudanese friends said:

Believe me, no child will be born unless he is surrounded by song.
No man will die without being surrounded by song. This is how we
turn our tragedy to triumph.

May that spirit of courage, determination and sheer joy fill all our hearts as we seek to fulfil the expectations of Africa.

Seizing the new millennium:
reshaping the world's economy

The Most Reverend Njongonkulu Ndungane,
Archbishop of Cape Town

In this extract from an address given at Southwark Cathedral in April 1997, Archbishop Ndungane makes the links between our responsibility as God's stewards, the obligations of the world of finance and the possibilities of new beginnings at the dawn of the new millennium. He begins with a general overview of the debt crisis, highlighting the poverty and environmental destruction that it has led to. He then calls for clear criteria for declaring debts odious and for an international Mediation Council to be established to deal with such debts. Finally he proposes nine principles by which future loans should be governed.

The history of developing countries and their relationship with the honey pots of the northern hemisphere is not happy. Many of these countries emerged from protracted freedom struggles against colonial oppressors and had to find their own feet economically. They grasped at economic lifelines thrown out by the developed countries. But the lifelines were flawed. Instead, the leaders of these countries incurred massive debts on behalf of their people – a people who were unaware that they were being dragged into a mire of foreign debt that would lead them into a sea of poverty.

In the 1960s, 1970s and 1980s, the world economy was dramatically reshaped as the rich nations lent money to the poor ones. The underlying tragedy is that the people of the poor nations had no understanding of the debt they were incurring any more than ordinary people of rich nations understand the intricacies of the world economy. The result is that millions of people in developing countries are now living in poverty while a massive transfer of wealth from the people of the south takes place to the developed and industrialised nations of the northern hemisphere. According to the United Nations, developing countries paid $1.662 trillion in servicing debt between the years 1980 and 1992 – three times the original amount owed in 1980. What is even more staggering is that despite this repayment, the total debt of developing countries is still estimated at more than $1.3 trillion.

This transfer is no accident. It is the result of a coherent set of decisions and forms part of a system of global relationships which reproduces the wealth–poverty dichotomy. Former French president, François Mitterand, was forced to admit at the G7 summit in Naples in 1994 that:

> *despite the considerable sums spent on bilateral and multilateral aid, the flow of capital from Africa towards the industrial countries is greater than the flow of capital from the industrial countries to the developing countries.*

The external debt of developing countries has become an eternal debt and stands as the largest immediate obstacle to growth and sustainable development.

Proclaim Liberty

It is important for us to understand the consequences of the iniqitous imbalance in the lives of ordinary people that results from this situation. The effects of poverty are wide-ranging and all-encompassing. Poverty imprisons individuals and whole communities, robbing them of their ability to live with dignity and self-respect. It is a curse which poses one of the greatest threats to society, undermining political stability, social cohesion and the environmental health of the planet. Poverty is a contributing factor towards the spread of diseases such as HIV and AIDS, internecine conflict and wars, and many environmental disasters.

Much of this poverty and environmental degradation is linked to the omnipresent black gold syndrome – oil. According to Helen Caldicott in her book *If You Love This Planet,* poor developing countries had, until 1973, made great strides in public health, preventive medicine and crop production. But then the OPEC countries suddenly increased the price of oil fivefold, and made huge profits by depositing their money in the world's major banks. The banks, ever eager to profit from this windfall, decided to offer low interest loans to Third World countries, which could obviously benefit from extra cash. The banks called this lending policy recycling, but it turned out to be an international lending spree in which they unloaded petro-dollars on unsuspecting developing countries. Tight monetary policies that followed, as a result of increasing deficits in the United States, saw interest rates double with a consequent rise in indebtedness by developing countries.

It is not only in the area of interest repayments that the powerful nations of the world control and restrict the development of others. Wealthy countries impose tariff or trade barriers on processed goods but seldom if ever on raw materials, thus ensuring that poor countries remain in poverty. To quote Caldicott again, in 1985 British tariffs on raw cotton were zero, on cotton yarn 8%, and on cotton T-shirts 17%. So the Third World can never break the poverty cycle because First World tariffs work against the importation of manufactured goods from the Third World.

The dire human consequences of these restrictive policies are complex. Governments have invested in arms, some rulers enriched themselves depositing their riches in Swiss and American banks, while the people ultimately responsible for the debt were swamped by malnourishment, famine and disease and in some cases war. And in so far as the environment is concerned, the World Bank encouraged countries to destroy tropical rainforests to repay their debts.

Stewardship and talents: the Christian response to debt
The Judaeo-Christian religion tells us that the world and all that is in it belong to the Lord (Psalm 24:1). As the Church we pay homage to God who is the Creator of heaven, earth and sea and all that is in them (Psalm 146:6). As followers of Christ, we have an onerous responsibility to act as faithful stewards of God's kingdom and his dominion over all, not to despoil the earth's resources, and not to be unjust in dealing with his creation. All of which means that we have to internalise in our personal, corporate and national lives the truth that 'when you have done it to one of the least of these you have done it to me' (Matthew 25:40).

The impact that debt has on restricting the ability of developing countries to grow can be interpreted in theological terms when one considers the parable of the talents. In this parable, Jesus speaks of how we are expected to use our talents and skills, to take the opportunities that are offered to us and to use them in the most productive way possible. Many of us are familiar with the story of the three servants, each of whom dealt with the money entrusted to him in a different way. One of them hid it under his bed, too scared to do anything with it, thereby earning the wrath of his master for having made no use of the opportunities presented to him.

Angela Tilby, in her address at Southwark Cathedral on Good Friday 1997, said that there are ways in which we oppress and imprison ourselves and each other, which prevent our gifts being used and block off the gift of the future. She adds:

Proclaim Liberty

One of the most effective ways of killing the future is by lending people things in such a way as to control them. In financial terms this is what the prosperous world did to many Third World countries when they had money to spare in the late 1970s. As a result, their economies are enslaved to ours. They have no future that is not in our interest. The God-given talents of millions of our fellow citizens are unable to flourish because they are being used to produce quick cash, simply to pay the interest on the loans. No one ever believes that the capital is repayable and so the rich nations have effectively turned the world into a slave economy.

We need to heed the lessons of Jesus in his talents parable as we are challenged to allow our brothers and sisters from poorer parts of the world to develop their gifts, free from the bondage of oppressive debt.

The situation in which developing countries find themselves is abhorrent. It cannot be acceptable to Christendom. Just as apartheid was unacceptable while some continued to justify it by the misuse of scripture, so the mounting debt of developing countries and the refusal to cancel this debt cannot be justified. God through Jesus Christ, and in the power of the Holy Spirit, reveals himself increasingly to us as our world unfolds. And, from a Church perspective, it should always be remembered that apartheid was declared a heresy because it flew in the face of our belief that every person is made in the image of God.

We are, of course, all conversant with the fact, also expressed in scripture, that one has to repay debts that have been incurred. As a general guiding principle, one can have little argument with this. When we think of debt, we tend to think of our own personal debts, our mortgages and outstanding loans. But there are striking differences between personal debts and the debts owed by governments. The main difference is this: our domestic bankruptcy laws enable us to draw a line under personal or commercial debts and bring them to an end. By drawing this line, these laws protect creditors from lending to bad debtors, but they also recognise that debt can destroy the lives of debtors, and so protect them accordingly. However, no such line can be drawn in international law. Yet, it is clear that where debts have been incurred without the concurrence of the debtor or where debts have grown to such a size that they could never be repaid, then a reshaping of the world economy is required.

In 1995, UNICEF called for the day to come:

> *when the progress of nations will be judged not by their military or economic strength, nor by the splendour of their capital cities and public buildings, but by the well-being of their peoples; by their levels of health, nutrition and education; by their opportunities to earn a fair reward for their labours; by their ability to participate in decisions that affect their lives; by the respect that is shown for their political and civil liberties; by the provision that is made for those who are vulnerable and disadvantaged; and by the protection that is afforded to the growing minds and bodies of their children.*

We can identify with this as a Church fully, not just because these are good values and results for which to strive, but because this is consistent with the biblical vision of jubilee – of a world where injustices are set right and the terrible poverty which we see portrayed on our televison screens and in our print media is diminished and ultimately eradicated. The jubilee vision is spelt out in Leviticus 25:8ff:

> *Consecrate the fiftieth year and proclaim liberty throughout the land to all its inhabitants ... For it is a jubilee and is to be holy for you; eat only what is taken directly from the fields ... Do not take advantage of each other, but fear your God (vv. 10, 12 and 17).*

We see the same strands of wisdom in Deuteronomy, in the first two verses of chapter 15:

> *At the end of every seventh year you are to cancel the debts of those who owe you money. This is how it is to be done. Everyone who has lent money to a fellow Israelite is to cancel the debt; he must not try to collect the money; the Lord himself has declared the debt cancelled.*

30

When debt is so severe that the poor and their rulers are prepared to mortgage the very tools of their livelihood, then a line must be drawn under the debts and the poor must be helped from falling deeper into the abyss of debt.

Odious debts and new mechanisms for international loans

As we approach the new millennium, the time has come to invoke the Doctrine of Odious Debt. This doctrine, which was first used almost 100 years ago by the United States, argues that where a debt has been incurred which is not in the interest of the State, but to strengthen a despotic regime to repress the population that fights against it, then it becomes odious to the population of the State. The debts of developing states which have arisen as a result of bad lending policies by the developed world should be declared odious and written off. Those debts incurred by colonial governments, corrupt governments or oppressive and illegitimate governments should also be declared odious.

South Africa is a prime example of an oppressive debt situation caused by governments that systematically oppressed the majority of its people. In 1973, the United Nations began to describe apartheid as a crime against humanity. Nevertheless, the international financial community, aided and abetted by the Nationalist Party government, continued to make loans to Pretoria, particularly in the critical 1980s, for which the new government is now held responsible. Clearly such loans were not in the interest of the majority of the people of South Africa nor in the interest of the people of sub-Saharan Africa, who were also affected to a greater or lesser extent by the grotesque policy of apartheid. Since South Africa's foreign debt, though comparatively small in relation to the overall debt, was incurred by and large under the apartheid regime, it should be written off. Most of its debt is owed to domestic sources, like banks and financial institutions, and creative ways must be found to restructure this debt.

It might seem that writing off debts is not financially realistic. But we should remember that while the sums owed by poor countries are large, when measured against the capital that flows in and out of the City of London each year they are the small change of the international financial exchanges. And lest I be accused of wanting sacrifices only from the industrialised nations, let me point out that in 1997 South Africa wrote off Namibia's debt to it, believing it effectively to be an odious debt incurred while Namibia was illegally occupied by the apartheid government.

Cancelling the debt of developing countries should not, however, be done without establishing a mechanism for its control and some important principles that will determine future economic relations between the rich and poor, thus contributing to peace, stability and prosperity. I therefore propose the establishment of a Mediation Council, whose responsibility will be to negotiate the repudiation of debts of developing countries. Such a council should consist of four parties, namely an independent international body, a similar regional body (for example, in the case of Africa, the Organisation of African Unity), the International Monetary Fund, and the country concerned. In addition, I propose the adoption of the following principles:

1. No country should be permitted to borrow more than a fixed percentage of its GNP (Gross National Product) without first going to its people, for example in a referendum, to obtain their approval. In this way, people and communities would be able to contribute to national debates as to whether they wish to incur international debt.

2. No debt should be incurred for the purposes of military expansion or arms purchases of any nature whatsoever or for maintaining oppressive governments that violate fundamental human rights.

3. Should a country expand its armed services or military capacity to the detriment of the development of its people, the international community should immediately cease all loans.

4. Preference should be given to making loans to countries which have illustrated good stewardship in the use of their resources and in the

Proclaim Liberty

involvement of their own people in their socio-economic development and the creative involvement of foreign investors.

5. Preference should be given to countries that need loans for health, education, social services, infrastructural development and the like.

6. The rape of the environment or the denial of human rights by any country should disqualify it from receiving loans.

7. A country which has shown a commitment to democratic government and regular free elections should receive preferential treatment in receiving loans.

8. Countries receiving loans from any international financial institution or commercial bank should submit themselves to a strict monitoring and accountability process so that if debt relief is used for military or other purposes that do not advance the socio-economic development of people, the loans be suspended.

9. This monitoring process must ensure that where a debt has been cancelled, any provision that would have been made to service the loan, had it not been cancelled, must be redeployed for the development of people and infrastructure.

The danger of such principles is that where a government ignores them, and has its loan called in, it is once again ordinary people who suffer the consequences. In such cases, the full weight of the Mediation Council and the international community should be brought to bear on the recalcitrant government, in much the same way as the apartheid regime was brought to its knees by international pressure.

Perpetuating the status quo cannot achieve the development needed in our global village in the next century. It will make poor countries poorer, and rich ones richer, with all the resultant threats to world peace that this involves. We must create models of hope that will give the vast majority of people in the world a new chance. We have a responsibility as we prepare for the next millennium to ensure that all people have the same opportunity to reach their full potential.

For this is a *kairos* moment: we are at the doorstep of the next one thousand years in the history of humankind. The first Christians stood on the threshold of the first millennium in a state of hopelessness after the crucifixion of Christ. But God raised him from the dead: hence our age is an age of hope, an age of new beginnings, an age of the Resurrection faith. It is applicable to everyone, from the multi-nationals of business to the multi-nationals of the Church. The opportunity to start anew must be seized. Through an act of immeasurable power and grace, let us grasp the nettle and reshape the world's economy.

In this way the third millennium can be a jubilee celebration and the Risen Lord can help us understand his proclamation 'Behold I make all things new!' and challenge us to join him in bringing new life and new hope to a dying world.

Debt relief for the Heavily Indebted Poor Countries:
the HIPC Initiative

Professor Sir Hans Singer

In 1996, the IMF, the World Bank and other multilateral creditors launched the Heavily Indebted Poor Countries (HIPC) Initiative to help solve the debt crisis of a group of countries which found themselves unable to confront their external debt burden. Two years later, the first beneficiaries are now receiving assistance under the Initiative. In this contribution, Hans Singer, one of the world's leading experts on development economics and the debt issue, provides economic background information on the debt crisis. This is followed by a description of the workings of the HIPC Initiative, and an evaluation of the Initiative's benefits and shortfalls.

The nature of the debt crisis

We may distinguish between a debt problem and a debt crisis. A debt problem has existed for a long time. For example as early as 1969 the Pearson Commission (chaired by Lester Pearson of Canada) gave this warning:

> *The accumulation of excessive debts is usually a combined result of errors of borrower governments and their foreign creditors. Failures on the part of the debtors will be obvious. The responsibility of foreign creditors is rarely mentioned.*

Since then the debt problem has developed into a debt crisis, particularly for the Heavily Indebted Poor Countries (HIPCs), mainly in Africa. A debt crisis means that these countries' debts are now recognised as unsustainable – that is to say, countries are unable to keep up the necessary flow of repayments on their debts.

This unsustainability has three aspects:

1. As a country's backlog of unpaid debt mounts up, so does *debt overhang* – the idea that an excessive debt burden deters investment, impedes growth and thus any chance of poverty reduction. A heavy overhang reduces the financial credibility of these countries. This in turn means that no foreign direct investment flows and higher interest is due on any loans received. Domestic investors, as a result, lose confidence and there is a constant threat of capital flight. Any new money received, meanwhile, is used to roll over existing debt, adding further to the overhang.

High debt overhangs mean increased risk for potential investors and hence less investment. Furthermore, when countries continually fail to service their debts at agreed levels and as their debt overhang increases, they are locked into a vicious cycle of exclusion from the global market and increasing poverty.

2. The servicing of the debt absorbs a high percentage of export earnings. This degree of unsustainability is illustrated by the fact that if the HIPCs had made all their scheduled debt payments during the 1985–1994 decade, no less than two-thirds of their total export earnings would have been used up. Even the actually paid debt, which was only 38% of the scheduled payments, absorbed over 22% of their export earnings. The corresponding figure for 1995 was still 20.4%, in spite of some recovery. And while in developing countries as a whole, the ratio of the debt stock to exports declined over the last few years to a perhaps sustainable level of 151%, in the HIPCs it stood at a clearly unsustainable level of 447%.[1]

Under the new HIPC Initiative, the sustainable proportion of export earnings absorbed by debt service (repayment of principal and payment of interest due) is put at 20% with anything over 25% clearly unsustainable. Yet even this represents a very heavy burden. It means that 20-25% of export earnings are not available for the import of developmental necessities, whether capital goods needed for investment and social infrastructure or consumer goods such as food or clothing. In the case of Mozambique, Oxfam considers a debt service to exports ratio of no more than 15% to be reconcilable with the goals of poverty reduction and overall economic sustainability.[2]

High levels of debt service act like a heavy tax on export earnings. This comes on top of a similar deterioration of 20-25% over the past few decades in terms of trade for primary products and low-tech manufactured goods – the main source of export earnings for the HIPCs. Such a double whammy is exacerbated firstly by the fact that most of the HIPCs are small countries (which always depend more on exports than large countries) with poor local markets; and secondly by the fact that much of the export trade of HIPCs is controlled by foreign investors and multinational corporations. This means that export earnings are not fully retained in the country but flow to the headquarters of the controlling corporations, usually located in the industrial countries.

The deteriorating terms of trade of the HIPCs have benefited those in the industrial countries as importers. They have been one element in helping to reduce and contain inflation. That factor alone justifies some special reciprocal action on the part of the creditors. Yet aid to these countries has been stagnant or declining. Between 1992 and 1996, for instance, official aid to developing countries from industrial countries and multilateral institutions fell by 16% in real terms.[3]

There has furthermore been an enormous instability of primary commodity prices to the order of 15% from one year to another. Because most HIPCs depend on a single or a very few primary commodities for export earnings, this makes it very hard to achieve macro-economic stability, let alone sustainable development. Research for 79 non-oil producing developing countries for the period 1970-1988 has shown that the 20 countries with the best terms of trade record have had significantly faster GNP growth than the 20 with the worst record (3.87% as against 3.21%).[4] Here lies one clue to ways of making debt service sustainable by better and more stable terms of trade.

3. Debt service absorbs a lot of scarce revenue which ought to be devoted to health, education, social infrastructure and other foundation stones for human and economic development. The high proportion of government revenue devoted to debt service does not sit well with the 20/20 compact agreed at the World Social Summit in Copenhagen of 1995, under which developing countries should devote 20% of their budget to poverty-reducing measures in health, education, sanitation, etc. All these factors come together to make the debt crisis of the HIPCs an insurmountable obstacle to their development and an essential factor in their increasing marginalisation and exclusion from the global economy. It means that debt relief for these countries must play a key role in any international agenda for a genuine fight against poverty and for making reality an all-inclusive global market with opportunities and potential benefits for all.

The HIPC Initiative

The HIPC Initiative was approved by the World Bank and IMF in September 1996. Its goal is the removal of debt burdens which pose an obstacle to development. It identifies 41 countries, 32 of them in Africa, where previous measures for debt relief had been insufficient. The bulk of these countries' debts are owed to official creditors, bilateral and multilateral.

The HIPC Initiative is an acknowledgement that proactive action by International Financial Institutions (IFIs) as well as national official creditors was required. It is also a tacit acknowledgement that previous multilateral programmes in the 1980s had led to cuts in precisely the kind of government investment in human capital and infrastructure that would have set this poorest group of countries on a path of growth and sustained development. Such development would have made their debts sustainable and provided an exit from debt rescheduling.

The HIPC, in spite of many limitations, represents a new approach to debt relief for a number of reasons:

1. The Initiative was adopted in late 1996 after the G7 had agreed that the Paris Club (representing the main bilateral creditors of the poorest countries) would provide up to 80% debt relief to countries receiving assistance under its auspices. This action by the Paris Club and subsequent attempts to improve the terms of the Initiative owed a great deal to the efforts of the British government. The Initiative is also greatly to the credit of the President of the World Bank, James Wolfensohn, who allocated $500 million as an initial contribution to the HIPC Trust Fund for debt relief.

All this represents a breakthrough, securing the participation of the multilateral IFIs – like the World Bank, IMF, Inter-American Development Bank, and Asian Development Bank – alongside bilateral creditors in the debt relief action. Such participation is an indirect recognition of the shared responsibility for the previous failure to create sustainable development, and to enable countries to service their debts fully. It also marks a more flexible attitude towards the 'absolute preferred creditor' status of the World Bank and IMF. This had been jealously guarded in order to maintain best possible access to capital markets for raising its finances, and it ruled out any overt debt relief on any of the loans made by these two organisations. At the end of the day, the HIPC Initiative is a recognition that there is a creditor problem as well as a debt problem and that for every unsustainable debt there must have been an unsustainable credit in the past.

2. There has also been a recognition of the need for greater transparency in giving aid, and in the lending practices of the multilateral institutions. This may pave the way for more independent evaluation, with a possible role for the non-governmental organisations (NGOs). It may also help to bring about procedures that are more genuinely based upon negotiation and agreement rather than imposition.

3. The HIPC Initiative is the first time that debt sustainability, and the debt relief required to achieve it, have been calculated according to a debt service/exports ratio. The link between the debt problem and the trade problems of poorer countries has often been ignored. But it is questionable whether the HIPC Initiative goes far enough in this regard. It is clear that a sustainable debt service/exports ratio must leave room for essential development needs to be met, and for poverty-reducing measures to be put in place, enabling the HIPCs to escape their marginalisation from the global community.

Ultimately, however, this requires larger measures, such as: an increase in the exports of poorer countries so that they can pay for social investment; a reduction in the instability of commodity prices in order to avoid sudden changes or sustained price deterioration wreaking havoc on poor countries' economies; and diversification of a country's export base. Finally, grant aid is necessary during the difficult transition to a truly sustainable situation.

There is another point to be made in this respect: debt/Gross Domestic Product ratios and debt service/export ratios are not sufficient guidelines for debt relief. They do not take account of how external factors affect export earnings, or of country-specific problems of economic and social development. But they are an essential beginning,

Proclaim Liberty

because they acknowledge the trap in which many of the poorest countries find themselves. 'Unsustainability' may sound better than insolvency, but if it is limited to a recognition that the nominal debt burdens incurred can never be paid under the present circumstances it avoids the main problem. The priority must be to restore the HIPCs to a solvent situation where they can make a new start and be able to take part in the flow of the world's resources, in such a way as to spread prosperity more evenly and increase foreign exchange earnings.

Weaknesses with the HIPC Initiative

There are several gaps in the HIPC Initiative which need to be addressed:

1. The details of the Initiative are highly complicated. In its original form, it called for a strict six-year time-frame, composed of two three-year probation periods. It also included tight criteria about the sound policies debtor countries had to pursue before they could become eligible for actual debt stock reduction and for debts to qualify as unsustainable. Only if a country passes six years of probation can it qualify for a reduction of up to 80% of its debt stock. The judgement about whether debtor countries qualify to obtain the HIPC benefits in full or in part would be largely based on an assessment by the Paris Club and the multilateral institutions.

There have been some signs of flexibility in the Initiative (most notably over allowing countries such as Uganda, Bolivia and Guyana to enter the second stage of probation straight away, and over taking fiscal constraints, and not just the size of exports into account when determining the ability to meet debt obligations). But there have also been criticisms. The UK has been among the countries pressing for further flexibility under the Mauritius Mandate. This Mandate recommends that by the year 2000 all eligible HIPCs should have at least made a start at receiving debt reduction and that three-quarters of the countries should have firm decisions about the amount and the terms of relief. The European Union's Development Commissioner, João de Deus

Pinheiro, meanwhile, has called for the HIPC Initiative to be more ambitious.

2. There is a clear need for more certainty about the exact criteria applied in judging a country's eligibility for HIPC assistance. Increased certainty is also paramount for assuring the populations of debtor countries, as well as domestic and foreign investors, that the promised assistance will be forthcoming at the agreed time, and in the right amounts. This makes it necessary to decide well in advance what amount of debt is owed to whom and how much of it should be cancelled by whom. Delays caused by member countries of the Paris Club wrangling over who should take responsibility for how much of the debt relief have been costly – not only in the literal sense. They have run the risk of creating uncertainty in the affected debtor countries and thus endangering any success in recent macro-economic consolidation.

3. There is a startling absence in the HIPC Initiative of any explicit targets for the reduction of poverty and of malnutrition. The HIPC Initiative should give the debt relief that enables countries to pursue pro-poor policies – which reduce poverty and malnutrition, discrimination and social exclusion. Both the IMF and World Bank have indicated that reduction of poverty, improvement in health, etc, will be taken into account in assessing full debt stock reduction. But it is important that pro-poor policies be given an equal footing to the sound economic policies demanded under World Bank and IMF Structural Adjustment Programmes.

4. Finally, it needs to be recognised that even should the debt burden be removed for these countries, many other obstacles to development remain. That is to say, the debt sustainability sought by the HIPC Initiative is a necessary but not sufficient condition for real development. And the HIPC Initiative should on no account be considered as an alternative to continued aid and investment. The myriad problems that poor countries face, such as political conflict, underqualified workforces, and lack of infrastructure, cannot be solved unless someone covers the

Proclaim Liberty

social investment required. If private investors will not, and domestic governments can not, then there is little alternative to foreign assistance. So international assistance is desirable not only for moral reasons. It also makes economic sense.

Concluding Remarks

There are a number of encouraging aspects of the HIPC Initiative, despite the fact that in some respects it still leaves much to be desired. We wish to conclude this chapter by summarising the positive and negative aspects of the new debt relief programme.

Good points:

- The Initiative comes at a time when special action is badly needed.
- It departs from the established habit of merely rescheduling debt, recognising the situation of insolvency in which many poor developing countries find themselves.
- It embraces the principle of debt cancellation in the cases covered by the Initiative and thus implicitly accepts joint responsibility for the accumulated debt burden.
- Multilateral debt has grown in relative importance in the case of HIPCs and this problem is finally being addressed.
- The original criteria for granting countries relief under the Initiative have often been handled with a substantial degree of flexibility. There is hope that this will be the case for some countries which have not yet been admitted.

Bad points:

- The robustness of the Initiative, that is, the debt stock reduction rather than debt rescheduling measures, may only become applicable after six years.
- The process for admitting a country to assistance under the Initiative is still long-winded and laborious.
- The criteria by which debt sustainability and eligibility are judged are exclusively financial ones. They should be supplemented by development criteria. HIPC assistance is still seen too much as a concession by creditor

countries, which impose conditions for relief on debtor countries.

To show full acceptance of the principle of joint responsibility for unsustainable debt, debtor countries should be fully incorporated into the process of deciding on financial assistance and policy design. What is needed is a new contract in which debtors and creditors join forces in an effort to overcome the debt crisis. There should be scope for HIPCs, creditor countries and multilaterals to work as partners towards a solution which is sustainable both financially as well as in the sense of providing a suitable basis for comprehensive development. The HIPC Initiative can be an important first step on the way to this target. One should remember, though, that a financially sustainable debt is not enough and that further efforts are needed to achieve comprehensive improvements which are built to last.

1. Figures based on the United Nations Conference on Trade and Development (UNCTAD) *Trade and Development Report*, 1997, pp 45-6.

2. Oxfam International, *Debt Relief for Mozambique: investing in peace*, 1997 (http://www.oneworld.org/oxfam/papers/moz97.html).

3. *The Economist*, February 14, 1998, p 128.

4. A.P. Thirwall, The Terms of Trade, Debt and Development: with particular reference to Africa, *African Development Review*, African Development Bank, June 1995.

44

Mzwakhe Nhlabatsi

The persistent problem of debt:
a gender perspective

Dr Agnes Abuom

The impact of debt upon women and gender relations is the subject of this contribution from Agnes Abuom, Director of the TAABCO Research and Development Consultants in Nairobi. She examines how women have suffered most from the debt crisis and particularly from structural adjustment programmes imposed to secure debt repayment. She explores this theme in the areas of food security, education, health and nutrition, and employment, particularly in the informal economy. She calls for Churches and non-governmental organisations to take concerted action to help and support the poor, and particularly women, affected by the debt crisis.

We live in a world that is polarised economically between countries and within them. The collapse of the bipolar political world following the demise of communism ushered in a spirit of triumphalism for capitalism. International economics have come to be dominated by finance capital – a process popularly referred to as globalisation. Although globalisation is not in itself destructive, its combination with a neo-liberal agenda has been. Globalisation has given market forces a free hand to run the economy, leading to a situation in which there is no economic justice, social and human costs are accepted as an inevitability, and ultimately inequality is institutionalised.

The persisting debt crisis must be seen as part of these wider economic processes. Debt and structural adjustment programmes (SAPs) continue to present a challenge to poor people, particularly women, and the Churches and organisations working for a more just society and sustainable development.

Africa's external debt-servicing poses a major obstacle to economic recovery. Africa's debt reached $322 billion in 1995, growing by almost 4% between 1994 and 1995, and representing 70% of the regional Gross Domestic Product and 250% of exports. Debt repayments absorb more than $10 billion annually. For Mozambique, Zambia and Tanzania, the repayment absorbs more than combined national budgets for primary health and primary education, and in some Heavily Indebted Poor Countries (HIPCs) in sub-Saharan Africa, scheduled debt servicing could absorb as much as 90% of total government revenue.

Third World economies have been forced to take remedial measures, through stabilisation programmes and Economic Structural Adjustment Programmes (ESAPs). The main aim of ESAPs has been to provide a cure for foreign debt through privatisation of state owned enterprises, reduction of government expenditures, and liberalisation of trade regimes. It was hoped that, as economies implemented these measures, foreign capital would be attracted by such deregulated markets, low wages and high interest rates.

Proclaim Liberty

These policies, however, have greatly increased poverty and marginalisation. They have led to increased inequality both within and between nations. Perhaps the most dramatic illustration of this is that the average life span of an African is 50 years – 14 years less than in South East Asia, 19 years less than in Latin America, and 24 years less than in industrial countries. These policies have also ensured that the role of the state over economic affairs is seriously eroded, while giving international financial institutions such as the IMF and World Bank sweeping powers over countries.

It is western countries, and particularly men from those countries, who form and implement economic policies, and hold economic power. It is clear that the IMF and World Bank policies were designed and also later modified to serve western economic interests. It is also clear that very few women participate at macro-economic decision-making levels, whether nationally or internationally. How has the debt crisis impacted differently upon men and women, and why?

The impact of ESAPs on gender relations

In Africa, ESAPs were specifically designed to solve the debt problem and to create economic growth. If they have led to greater social disintegration, poverty, unemployment, reduced consumption, lower levels of education and deteriorating public health, then they are manifestly failing to achieve their original goal. Women bear the brunt of the negative effects of these programmes, and the economic policies that come with them, particularly in five main areas: food security, education, health, employment, and the informal economy.

Food security

According to the Food and Agriculture Organisation (FAO), food security has deteriorated in sub-Saharan Africa during the past 25 years. Between 1969 and 1992, the proportion of people without adequate food rose from 38 to 43% and the absolute number of hungry people doubled from 103 million to 215 million. About 30% of African children are malnourished, and out of the 82 countries classified by the FAO as Low Income Food Deficient Countries, 41 are in Africa making the continent the most food insecure region in the world.

Women are most affected by food insecurity. In many Third World countries, boys are favoured to girls and this is reflected in eating habits. Women, especially in Africa, are the last to eat, making them more vulnerable to food shortages. They are also often prohibited by cultural taboos from eating food nutritionally beneficial to their reproductive health eg eggs, chicken, etc.

Yet it is women who are the main producers of food, especially in Africa. This enormous responsibility is carried out despite numerous problems, some directly related to ESAPs. In most cases, women have no access to credit facilities. Economic liberalisation, meanwhile, brought about by ESAPs, has led to the removal of tariffs for imported agricultural products, leading to the flooding of domestic Third World markets with cheap western agricultural exports, and a decline in the domestic market.

ESAPs have also oriented economies towards export products. Even though it is usually women who produce export oriented commodities, it is men in most cases who own them and receive the income. Rural development programmes, meanwhile, have tended to focus on men and not women, and export crops rather than food crops.

Food security is the minimum that human life needs to survive, and currently this is not possible for millions of households. Agricultural and economic policies condemn poor men and women to death. The Bible states that 'Thou shall not kill/commit murder' yet we have policies that kill women and children daily.

Education
Cuts in government spending on education have led to a growing gap between the literate and illiterate. Literacy rates in the Third World are generally low compared to the First. African ones are among the lowest in the world. Half of all African adults are illiterate, while female literacy is

38%. School enrolment for girls is substantially lower than for boys. African school enrolment figures are less than half the average of the Latin American and Asian, hence the phenomenon of street children, and high drop-out rates particularly among girls. A quarter of Uganda's 200,000 primary school children, for instance, drop out each year.

The cost of education has become very expensive in the face of the ESAPs in the 1990s. Faced with school fees, parents often give preference to boys while girls are withdrawn to assist with household chores or to be married. Financial hardship in rural areas means that there are comparatively few girls in secondary school. The same is true for university enrolment. There are, furthermore, negative attitudes towards girls' involvement in science and technical subjects, and a perpetuation of gender stereotypes in the curriculum.

According to the World Health Organisation (WHO), some 10 million street children worldwide are engaged in begging, stealing, prostitution and drug abuse. Many of these are girls who have fled physical and emotional abuse in employment as housemaids, and for whom the street becomes the best option. The implications of children living on the street are a serious threat to the stability of society.

In summary, boys are still privileged compared to girls. This is why the Beijing Platform of Action for girls needs to be implemented by Churches, NGOs and governments. The Churches are not completely exempt from the gender biases. Even though the Church teaches that 'in Christ there is no Jew nor Gentile, slave nor free, male nor female' (Galatians 3:28), they have not fully addressed the issue of gender, and the biblical images of women they use have often been negative ones.

Health

ESAPs have led to a cut in non-productive social spending. Due to this, health budgets have fallen drastically. The World Bank proposes privatisation of health services and cost-sharing – a prescription that leaves no provision for the poor and vulnerable. The scenarios of poor mothers with children and men queuing for places in hospitals is common everywhere.

Such budget reductions have led to the deterioration of health services, with devastating effects on the status of women. Women have special health needs due to their reproductive functions, their generally longer life expectancy and their role as caretakers of family health. Maternal mortality rates are very high now in Africa, and appear to be rising. Lack of adequate medical facilities is the biggest contributing factor to this high mortality rate. In parts of rural Africa, 50% of women who start childbearing at 16 or 17 die by the age of 50 from fertility-related causes. Perhaps even more striking is the fact that 25% of all African women between ages 15-45 are pregnant each year, compared to less than 10% of the industrialised world. These figures reflect the need for family planning services which at present reach only 10% (8 million) women in sub-Saharan Africa largely due to economic hardships.

With the collapse in the health system for the poor, women have to cope with caring for the aged sick, the children and other ill members of the family. Moreover, their own health is in jeopardy because of their critical roles of economic production and childbearing. The AIDS epidemic has put added pressure on women. The theological position of some Churches on the use of contraceptives has not taken account of the vulnerability of women to AIDS. What does a woman who is threatened by AIDS do when she cannot protect herself, and what is the meaning of 'What God has put together, let no man put asunder' in such situations?

The measures proposed by the IMF and World Bank have led to a two-tier system in which the rich visit the flourishing private health sector, and the poor, especially women and disabled people, are simply unable to meet their health needs.

Employment
The neo-liberal programme implemented through ESAPs has weakened national economies, making them more vulnerable to international

investors. Public sector lay-offs, although designed to increase efficiency and reduce government spending, have led to unemployment, job insecurity, and a rise in crime rate. In countries where major restructuring has been undertaken (eg Uganda and Kenya), women have usually been the first to be laid off – 'the last to be hired and the first to be fired' – often with excuses such as maternity leave not being conducive to industrial productivity.

Even if it is their husbands who are laid off, women are still the ones who have to come up with coping mechanisms and ways to rescue the situation. As roles change in the household, there has also been an increase in domestic violence as well as general violence against women. It is not surprising that diseases formerly associated only with men, such as high blood pressure, diabetes and heart attacks, are becoming common among women.

The Bible teaches that we should support ourselves from the labour of our hands. We are created as co-workers with God. Yet massive unemployment and underemployment abound. What human dignity is left for the people who have been puked out by an economic system that has no value for their livelihood and no use for their labour? In many countries, Churches have lost contact with labour to such an extent that when globalisation squeezes trade unions, they have no message.

The informal sector

The informal sector is the fastest growing sector in Third World economies. With the jolt of ESAPs this sector has sprouted very fast in major urban centres and rural markets. In this sector, women tend to occupy themselves with petty trading of food stuffs. Men engage in more lucrative areas such as hardware and manufactured goods. Petty trade allows women to combine child care and economic activity, and in any case, few women have access to the capital needed to carry out more lucrative business.

In Kenya, as in most Third World countries, women make up the majority of those selling used clothes *(mitumba)* and food stuffs in the rural market. The central business districts of many towns are also filled with women sitting on pavements in the roasting sun, with young children dangling from their backs, selling their wares. These horrible conditions are not made any better by constant harassment from the police. The authorities are unable to provide proper sheds, and when they do, most hawkers are not able to pay rental fees.

The involvement of women and men in this sector results from lack of other economic oportunities. Within this informal sector there is also much illicit trade. This is a big sector in Latin America where retrenched workers have moved into cocaine production in rural areas, the profits from which go to drug barons rather than benefiting the poor. Other illicit activities include child and adult prostitution, illegal brewing and other criminal acts such as bank robberies.

While the market thrives on individuals profiting at the expense of communities, the poor and marginalised are holding fast to the culture of solidarity and reciprocity. Urban and rural poor have, against all odds, persisted in organising for survival. It is usually the women who stand as pillars against the violence unleashed by the market forces. Women's organisations have faced an uphill task, however, confronting manipulation and exploitation by men, especially politicians. This has also been true in the Church. Despite the fact that women form the economic backbone of the Church, using their limited resources accrued from petty trade, they are rarely involved in the decision-making processes and tend to be marginalised.

Moral obligations for debt repayment

The debt crisis and the harsh conditions imposed by the IMF and the World Bank have hit women hardest. Poverty amongst women in sub-Saharan Africa and in the Third World in general, is now greater than ever before. Few of the projects undertaken in the 1980s and early 1990s with the loans were of direct benefit to poor people, owing to corruption and misappropriation. Due to their distance from political and economic centres of decision-making, the poor have little clue as to what the debt is about. All they know is that their lives are growing worse and worse.

Proclaim Liberty

One is therefore bound to pose the question: Why should women suffer most in repaying the debts that they least benefited from? In some countries – Central America, Ethiopia, Liberia, Somalia, Uganda, Sudan and the DRC (formerly Zaire) – money borrowed was used to finance military expenditure on a massive scale, with devastating effects on the civilian population, particularly women and children.

The sacrifice of human lives to market forces continues, as does the exclusion and marginalisation of the majority of people from any engagement in socio-economic and political decision-making processes. It is surely unethical to continue to demand repayments from poor people while the rich continue to thrive and grow richer. An economic system that condemns millions to death should no longer be accepted.

Conclusion

The debt crisis continues with its unabated negative impact on the poor, especially women. With the process of globalisation, women find even the limited spaces they had carved out threatened by market forces. Current economic structures have shown little regard for people – especially for the values and cultures of poor men and women. These structures have singularly failed to guarantee life.

Due to the debt crisis, the Third World is still engulfed by abject poverty, persistent civil wars, gender disparities, institutional mismanagement and corruption, poor economic performance, disease, illiteracy and unemployment. Moreover, it is apparent that none of these problems can be solved by an individual country, community or agency. Rather, they require a coordinated and collaborative international approach by all stakeholders concerned.

The NGOs, Churches, and other faith communities need to make a concerted effort in addressing debt relief and cancellation. This will require advocacy and lobbying work with the governments of the West, as well as with the international financial institutions. The poor need a reliable voice to relay their cry to the powers that be, to carry the message that economic policies are strangling them. Faced with economic and social values that are against life, the Churches are called upon to facilitate the organisation of communities and to promote the values of social justice, peaceful co-existence and respect for human and basic rights, especially those of women and indigenous people.

This is the time to act. The Church is called to be a witnessing, serving and prophetic community and to take up economic issues as a matter of faith.

The biblical jubilee:
political economy and Christian realism

Dr Pat Logan

In this piece,* the history and context of the biblical concept of jubilee are explored by Pat Logan, who is Social Responsibility Adviser for the Kingston Episcopal Area and Housing and Homelessness Adviser for the Diocese of Southwark. He does so in order to assess how it can be used in campaigning for debt relief today. He argues that despite some real difficulties – not least that the Jubilee was a top-down response to poverty and indebtedness, and does not appear ever to have been enacted – there is a realism at the heart of the jubilee message which makes it a very strong symbol for understanding, and seeking to solve, the present debt crisis.

*Adapted from an article for the Milton Keynes and Malvern papers

Proclaim Liberty

Jubilee 2000 and the biblical jubilee

Invoking the biblical jubilee as the framework for the current campaign to ease the burdens of heavily indebted countries is not as straightforward as it might seem. A close examination of the biblical jubilee (Leviticus 25:8-55) confronts us with at least four major difficulties. The most embarrassing of these is that the jubilee year is not primarily concerned with debt but with the restoration of land and the release of slave labour; provisions for debt relief are the concern of the Sabbath Year.[1] A second difficulty presented by the biblical jubilee is that it was not a movement from below, but rather an instrument designed by the priestly and upper classes more for the purpose of enhancing their legitimacy than for transferring power. The third difficulty with the biblical jubilee is that it called for an unconditional restoration of property and freedom, an approach which would, at least on the surface, appear to be both unjust and irresponsible. The final difficulty is that it simply did not work and never really took hold.

It would be easy but mistaken to conclude that, therefore, the jubilee theme is inappropriate for the current campaign for debt relief. Deeper examination of the background and meaning of the biblical jubilee reveals at least four very important strengths in the jubilee theme, which more than offset the weaknesses mentioned above. It shows, first, that the jubilee theme helps set the question of debt in a wider framework of economic activity. Secondly, that its grounding in political realism makes it more not less relevant to the state of our political economy today. Thirdly, that it takes us beyond our all-too-common individualist and purely formal concepts of justice and directs us towards the common good. And fourthly, that the jubilee symbol retains the moral and spiritual power to inspire hope and to shape action.

a) The biblical jubilee and the restoration of land

In calling for the restoration of land, the jubilee year legislation was much more radical than the Sabbath year legislation (Deuteronomy 15), which called only for the release of debts. Being in debt need not lead to financial ruin nor to slave labour as long as a person managed to hold onto their land (an important income-generating asset). Being without land meant being without hope since gone would be the means of repaying any debt which might then be incurred. Creditors were not slow to appreciate the difference.

Land was the central factor throughout most of the history of Israel. In an agrarian economy, land represented more than a place on which to dwell or a form of investment. It was the basic means of production and of people's livelihood. It determined not just status but class, not just consumption but wealth. To affirm that the land belonged ultimately to God was not just one article of faith amongst many. It was a core belief with profound practical implications.

But the land question assumed special importance when Israel's exile in Babylon was drawing to a close and her elite were preparing to return home. In their absence, much of their land had been distributed to others. A new chapter in the people's history meant the need for a new constitution, and for the land issue to be at the centre of it. That is why the jubilee legislation, which was drawn up at that time, was placed deliberately and firmly within the Code of Holiness (Leviticus 17-26).

b) The biblical jubilee and political realism

Looking at the biblical jubilee from the perspective of Christian realism brings to light a fascinating interplay of interest groups, ideologies and power relationships.[2] The jubilee legislation must be placed in the wider context of other practices of release from debt or slave-labour, adopted in the Ancient Near East, later Mediterranean civilisations and even Israel itself.

Shrewd rulers always appreciate the limits of their power. They know the importance of portraying themselves as preservers of order, even as champions of justice, and of persuading their subjects that the order over which they preside is divinely ordained. This is what makes successful systems of exploitation so remarkably stable. Yet such systems are still prone to crises of various sorts – created by internal economic contradictions, power struggles within the ruling class, and external factors such as threats of foreign invasion, or opportunities for conquest. Each such crisis places a strain on the relationship between ruler and ruled. And among the measures which shrewd rulers may adopt to ease the pressure and to preserve the system are practices of release. These, then, come essentially not from below but from above, and are more often conservative than revolutionary.

The most famous example in classical times was the cancellation of debt and abolition of debt slavery by the Athenian statesman, Solon, in 594 BC – just decades before the jubilee legislation itself. Solon, a member of the landed gentry known for his justice, was the ruling class choice to instigate reforms in the face of popular unrest arising from the burden of debt. There are other, earlier examples of practices of release arising at crisis points:

• The Sumerian Prince Urukagina (c.2400-2350 BC), who decreed debt release to the people of Lagesh, appears to have been a usurper seeking to gain legitimacy.

• In the Old Babylonian Kingdoms of Isin (2017-1794 BC) and Larsa (2025-1763 BC), new kings marked their accession by issuing a partial amnesty (*misarum*).

• The neo-Assyrian practice of debt-release (*andurarum*), such as the edict of Ammisaduga, King of Babylon (c.1646-1624 BC), may have been an attempt to recruit people for military service and persuade them to make sacrifices in defence of their country.

Israel's rulers, too, resorted to practices of release, thus furnishing precedents on which the jubilee legislation drew. The Sabbath-year regulations for the remission of debt and the release from slavery (Deuteronomy 15) are an example of such practices becoming legislation. Most such practices came in the monarchical period and were decrees by individual kings. Martin Chaney, for instance, suggests that the law requiring the freeing of one's Hebrew slave in the seventh year (Exodus 21:2) may reflect Jeroboam I's need to legitimate his secession from Judah.[3]

He also suggests that Jehu's relaxing of debt may have been a means of legitimating his coup, and that Josiah may have used debt remission and release from slavery to erode the power-base of corrupt elites. The remission of slavery by Zedekiah, meanwhile, according to Niels Peter Lemche, could have been a measure to attract recruits in the struggle against Babylon.[4]

These measures, however, limited rather than eliminated the practices of slavery and debt, which were themselves accepted as legitimate.

c) Political realism and the legislators of the jubilee

We have already seen how important it was to resolve the question of land redistribution at the time of return of Israel's elite from exile. But in the absence of a monarchy, who was to decide, on what authority, and with what criteria?

The sort of settlement needed was one which incorporated both a spirit of renewal and an element of restoration of the position of those who had been in exile. Who better than the priests, who claimed to speak with divine authority whilst also enhancing their own interests? They alone were in a position to act both as interpreters of God's action and as legislators of God's will. But, as Jeffrey Fager describes in fascinating detail, there were two priestly factions, both stressing the centrality of the land question and both advocating differing versions of theocracy.[5]

The minority Ezekielian faction championed the more radical, utopian vision. Basing their claims on direct revelation rather than law, they envisioned a new age and a new cosmic order. That new order involved a fundamental redistribution of land. Opposing them was the majority priestly faction, whose views found expression in the jubilee legislation. Theirs was the more conservative proposal. Although their jubilee proposals did not stand the test of time, they showed considerable political realism – appealing to people in terms of their own Sinaitic traditions; redistributing land to all, and thus checking the emergence of rival power groups; and finally, acknowledging that injustice existed even amongst the restored people of Israel and needed to be provided for in law. In all of this, the jubilee legislation sought not so much to abolish but to contain economic injustice.

d) The biblical jubilee as faith and ideology

Rulers have often recognised that to maintain power they need to legitimise their rule in the eyes both of the masses and their internal rivals. That legitimation, until the advent of the modern era, usually rested on a set of beliefs which were religious as well as ethical.[6] Such beliefs were deeply rooted in the daily lives and folk memories of the people. They helped make up the rich and complex notions of justice, setting the parameters beyond which only foolish and arrogant rulers would stray. True, rulers used such beliefs to construct their ideologies, but though they refashioned and rearranged them, they did not create them.

Thus it was with the jubilee. The priests fashioned it but were also its instruments. They had to ground it in people's daily experience and cherished beliefs. Even the 50-year cycle had a grounding in experience, representing at once the moment for a new generation to emerge, a tried and tested practice of lease-hold in Babylon, and the historical time frame of the Exile itself (587-538 BC). But, ultimately, the jubilee appealed to the memory of God's intervention in the lives of his people, especially with the Exodus, and to the idea of a just God who had led his people from captivity into a promised land. Liberation theology it was not, but it did keep alive faith in a liberating God.

In the end, the jubilee legislation did not take hold. This was due in part to its lack of practicality, and to the fact that the priests were not able to enforce the law since in the restored Israel power resided with Persian, Hellenistic and, later, Roman overlords. Furthermore, the restored Israel was entering a period when trade and commerce were becoming important. Money rather than land was becoming the driving force of the economy. And in that sort of economy, the 50-year restoration of land was simply not practicable.

Yet the jubilee theme continued to survive, sometimes in bizarre and apocalyptic modes, even if the legislation itself did not. It is even possible to see Jesus' own manifesto (Luke 4:18-19) as part of that faith.[7] What is beyond doubt is that the practice of release central to Jesus' message of grace and forgiveness was part of the Gospel of a liberating God. Like the jubilee release, Jesus' offer of freedom was unconditional and a matter of grace, not merit. The age of scarcity had given way to the age of abundance.

Conclusion: Jubilee 2000 – grounds for hope?

Why then should we use the theme of jubilee to attempt to bring about social change? The advantages of the jubilee theme stem from its radicalism, its realism and its symbolic power. How does this relate to the campaign to relieve world debt?

1. The biblical jubilee provides an appropriate framework for the Jubilee 2000 campaign because, paradoxically, it helps us avoid the mistake of seeing debt as the central issue. Debt is not *per se* an evil. Borrowing can be good for consumers, for small businesses and for the economy as a whole. It can even be good for national economies, if used to promote the development of a nation's infrastructure and social capital.

Borrowing becomes harmful when it takes place within vastly unequal power relationships, and when repayment by poor people and countries involves enormous hardship. Under such conditions debt becomes a vicious and morally objectionable mechanism for reinforcing dependency and deepening exploitation.

It is one of the merits of the biblical jubilee that it invites us to look beyond debt to more fundamental economic realities, such as land and labour. The Jubilee 2000 campaign is likely to be more successful in bringing about true jubilee justice if it too directs attention to some of the deeper flaws in our economic structures, including the huge gaps between rich and poor, the lack of accountability of transnational corporations and global financial institutions, and the vulnerability of labour.

2. But if credit and debt play an important and positive role in contemporary economic activity, so do mechanisms for controlling debt. Over-indebtedness can put a brake on the entire economy, leading to reduced consumption, increased unemployment, lower profits and, in some contexts, political instability. Here we enter the world of realism which characterises the biblical jubilee.

With the demise of communism, capitalism has, for the moment, no rivals. These are not revolutionary times. For that very reason, while it is more important than ever to stand alongside the poor, any major contemporary practice of release, whether it be land redistribution, debt cancellation or abolition of slave-labour, must come from the top.

There are sound arguments, based on political realism, that it is in the interests of global capitalism to employ a practice of release by easing the burden of heavily indebted countries. To do so is good for business and good for political stability. Good for business because unsustainable debt means economic stagnation, as investment dries up and trade suffers. Good for political stability, because it could prevent internal unrest and religious fanaticism in less developed countries and thence in the world in general.

3. The third advantage of the jubilee theme is that its concept of justice transcends the individualism promoted by markets, and embedded in prevailing versions of democracy. The jubilee theme points us rather, when applied to the debt crisis, towards the promotion of the common good.

4. The jubilee also has a powerful spiritual and ethical appeal. For believers in the story of a liberating God, it is a summons to express faith and to accept discipleship. As Sharon Ringe puts it: 'The power of these images [of the Jubilee] helps us say what it means to confess Jesus as the Christ.' [8] For those who do not believe the story, the jubilee also has an ethical appeal, not least because the present state of world debt is ultimately an issue of justice.

The architects of the biblical jubilee were not the prophets but the priests. So, too, it is today's priests, bishops and archbishops who are ideally placed to mediate between the powerless and the powerful and to show where common interest lies. The system does, however, need to be changed radically. But the prospects for doing so are hardly favourable at the moment. What is possible is something more modest, as the jubilee

62

itself was. The burdens of the poor can be lifted. The nightmare of debt without end can be dispelled. The time is right, for three reasons:

First, the collapse of communism has opened up a new period which challenges us to find other ways of constraining and guiding economic power.

Second, the jubilee's principle of self-limitation is the sort which is increasingly important in our age of risk and reflexivity. The time span prescribed by the jubilee, that is, 50 years, might be an appropriate marker for the economic and political powers to commit themselves to a radical economic audit for the sake of the next generation.

Third, the original jubilee legislation was framed at a turning point in world history – the sixth century BC – as religious and social movements emerged throughout the Mediterranean, the Near East and the Indian sub-continent. Might it not be that the renewal of the jubilee spirit in our own times is a sign that we too may be on the threshold of a new stage in human history?

1. Raphael Jospe, Sabbath, Sabbatical and Jubilee: Jewish ethical perspectives, and Leon Klenicki, Jewish Understandings of Sabbatical Year and Jubilee, in Hans Ucko, ed., *The Jubilee Challenge: utopia or possibility?* Geneva: World Council of Churches, 1997.
2. Patrick Logan, *Biblical Reflections on the Political Economy of Jubilee*, Southwark Diocesan Board for Church in Society, 1997.
3. Martin Chaney, Debt Easement in Israelite history and tradition, in David Jobling, Peggy I Day and Gerald Sheppard, eds., *The Bible and the Politics of Exegesis: essays in Honor of Norman K. Gottwald on his sixty-fifth birthda*, Cleveland, Ohio: Pilgrim Press, 1991.
4. Niels Peter Lemche, The Manumission of Slaves: the fallow year – the sabbatical year – the jubilee year, in *Vetus Testamentum* 26 (January 1976), pp 38-59.
5. Jeffrey A. Fager, Land Tenure and the Biblical Jubilee: uncovering hebrew ethics through the sociology of knowledge, *Journal for the Study of the Old Testament*: Supplement Series 115, Sheffield Academic Press, 1993.
6. A penetrating examination of the various ways in which political power is legitimised is offered by David Beetham, *The Legitimation of Power*, London: Macmillan, 1991.
7. Christopher Wright in the *Anchor Bible* maintains that Luke 4 does refer to the jubilee; Michael Prior, in *Jesus the Liberator: Nazareth Liberation Theology*, Sheffield Academic Press, 1995, says it is doubtful, while Anthony Harvey and Leslie Houlden (private correspondence) deny it altogether.
8. Sharon Ringe, *Liberation and the Biblical Jubilee*, Philadelphia: Fortress Press, 1985, p 36.

Proclaim Liberty

The ethics of debt:
a theological appraisal

Professor Canon John S. Pobee

In this piece, John Pobee, a distinguished ecumenical theologian from Ghana, currently on the staff of the World Council of Churches, explores some theological concepts with which to respond to the debt crisis. It is an extract from a paper presented at the WCC consulatation on debt in Malaga, Spain, in April 1998. In it he argues for the creation of an ecumenical ethic. He calls for such an ethic to be based on the idea that God is the Creator and Creditor of us all. This ethic would measure what is good by what is human, would be the basis for the creation of a community of communities based on solidarity and sharing, and would express God's preferential option for the poor.

As we prepare for the turn of the millennium, we are all too conscious that world debt seems to belie the Church's proclamation of salvation and redemption of all creation. The debt crisis challenges our religious and ecumenical vocation as the people of God, the Creator of the whole world. Thus, although, the debt issue is of course an economic and political concern, it is also a religious and spiritual one. Under the canopy of jubilee and the turn of the millennium, we are offered the opportunity to learn from how things have gone wrong and to seek to stop the looming Gadarene rush to self-destruction. These symbolic moments are, among other things, occasions for taking stock of life, and for exploring how we can begin to build peace and security for the global community.

The significance of the jubilee motif for today

The jubilee motif of the Old Testament calls for three major things: *ecological integrity and liberation* (Leviticus 25:12); *justice and peace* (Lev. 25:13-23); and *stewardship and solidarity with the poor* (Lev. 25:23-55). The jubilee was not just some religious calendar to be ticked off. It had everything to do with national life, with the quest for peace and justice, with the ecological and socio-economic imbalance in the world.[1]

These themes are just as relevant today as they were in Israelite society, despite the fact that the concept of debt in the Old Testament is different from that of our own day. In Israel, debt was articulated with social organisation and hierarchy, and rooted in the kinship practices of reciprocity and gift exchange. Today's concept of debt is much more economic, and based on the political economy of market-exchange, and accumulation of economic power through the appropriation of natural resources.

The jubilee motif continued beyond the Old Testament. Jesus' first sermon at Nazareth (Luke 4:17-21) picked up the jubilee theme, proclaiming the Kingdom of God, the remission of debts and the liberation of slaves. The ministry and mission of Jesus was, and still is, a call to us to be a jubilee people.

Proclaim Liberty

For Christians today, the Bible is the word of life. The faith which we proclaim is not an esoteric, ethereal thing; it has to do with real things, with life in abundance. The Russian theologian Nicolai Berdyaev stated the Christian position when he said:

The question of bread for myself is a material question, but the question of bread for my neighbours, for everybody, is a spiritual and a religious question. Man does not live by bread alone but he does live by bread and there should be bread for all. Society should be so organised that there is bread for all, and then it is that the spiritual question will present itself before men [and women] in all its depth: it is not permissible to base a struggle for spiritual interests and for a spiritual renaissance on the fact that for a considerable part of [humankind] bread will not be guaranteed ... Christians ought to be permeated with a sense of the religious importance of the elementary daily needs of people, the vast masses of people, and not to despise these needs from a sense of exalted spirituality.[2]

The debt crisis denies a considerable part of humanity their daily bread. This is the bottom line of the faith approach to debt. The debt crisis most affects those who are already excluded and disadvantaged. And it is this which makes it an ethical issue, a matter of faith. What we need in dealing with it is an ethic which seeks to ensure peace, security, justice and dignity for all, especially those on the margins. The jubilee offers just such an ethic.

A theological appraisal of debt

1. The one creator God of us all – God the greatest creditor

Africa's wisdom is couched in proverbs. One such proverb of the Akan of Ghana states: 'We are, each and all, God's children and no one may be treated as a child of this earth.' That proverb affirms what the Bible also affirms, namely the one Creator God, the heart of the ecumenical vocation. It also goes on to draw the conclusion that for precisely this reason no one may be excluded or disenfranchised.

Precisely because we are each and all God's creation and children, we are each and all debtors to God (Matthew 18:23-35) who makes His rain fall on the just and unjust. The parable of the unmerciful servant has some interesting challenges for us. A king had his servants under him, one of whom owed him a debt of colossal size. When he could not pay, his debt was not merely deferred until payment was possible, but was remitted altogether. The same steward could not extend such generosity to a fellow servant who owed him a lesser debt.

This parable may not be taken literally but it states some Christian positions which I wish to lay out here and which challenge us as we engage with the issue of debt:

• Whites and blacks, North and South, male and female – all are part of God's creation. Yet the way blacks have been treated by colonialists, racists and slave owners means that even the affluent North owes a great debt to God. Nations of the North got rich because they exploited the peoples of the South. That is the starting-point of the debt discussion for us Christians – we are all in one way or other debtors to the one Creator God of all.

• Forgiveness is not so much an act as an attitude. It does not matter how often forgiveness is needed. The crucial thing is a forgiving disposition. Do our creditors in the North have a forgiving disposition which does not count the number of times? Seventy times seven says the Scripture. What does this say to our creditors?

• The greatest Creditor, God, does not wait for debtors to fulfil all conditions. Even the greatest debtor is forgiven.

• At the bottom of the issue of debt remission, then, is the quality of generosity – the unreserved forgiveness by the Creditor.

• Forgiveness is not one sided. It is not something to be offered by the injured party. The concern should be for the restoration of relationships between members of God's household, between debtors of the greatest Creditor.

Is it possible to live this out in the modern world? If I may use a biblical expression, 'It is a hard saying.' The Bible offers us a challenge because we claim our faith is nurtured on Scripture.

2. What is human is the measure of the good

The late Dietrich Bonhoeffer has a challenge for us: 'To be a Christian does not mean to be religious in a particular way, to make something of oneself (a sinner, a penitent or a saint) on the basis of some method or other, but to be human.'[3] The Bible speaks of humanity as being made in the image and likeness of God. To be human is to have dignity, to be compassionate and just, and to share in God's creative work. The creditor like the debtor is called to join in God's creative work which, as Scripture puts it, was good.

From that point of view, the debt issue is about whether the measures in place foster that image and likeness of God in the peoples of the South, as of the North. Evaluation of IMF and World Bank recipes for southern countries should be evaluated in this light. Do the ideas and ideologies informing the discussion of the debt crisis take seriously the question of what is human? Bishop Selby describes the debt crisis thus:

> *When we come to examine debt in a global context we are confronted not just by debt, the debilitator of people's lives, but by debt as a serial and multiple killer ... It puts the poorest of the world against one another in a struggle for what remains of the world's resources after the insatiable appetite of the world's debt economy has devoured their much-needed substance. But ... again, it is not sufficient to pay attention to the plight of the victims of global indebtedness, desperate as that often is, it is the world's creditors, not just its debtors, who need to be considered.*[4]

These comments add up to the fact that economic factors and religious factors have a meeting point in what is human. The project of progress is to be judged by whether it fosters what is human.

3. Building a community of communities

The eurocentric world is finished; the model of centre-periphery for organising the world community of peoples is finished. We need a new model, a new ideology, a new ethic to organise our common sharing of the one world created by the greatest Creditor of all, God. Several institutions exist today which suggest that we now seek our common security in community – for example the UN and the Organisation of African Unity. The very talk of globalisation[5] tends also in that direction. We have now become more conscious that we live in a global village, thanks to the communications revolution. So the issue is not whether to globalise or not; it is rather how we measure the present model of globalisation by what is human.

The ecumenical movement uses a key word *koinonia* (Greek) or *communio* (Latin) in its discussions. This is the basic understanding of the Church: but it has more significance and ramifications than just intra-church activity. The root meaning of the word is participation, and *koinonia-communio* is translated and expressed by such words as communion, fellowship, solidarity, sharing. How do we express solidarity between the different nations, races, tribes, languages, genders and ages around debt, however? For those of us who enter the discussion from an ecumenical angle, the ideal of *koinonia* is not an option but an imperative because we affirm that the earth is the Lord's and all that is in it (Psalm 24:1) and because we share in the life of God, the Trinity.

The word communion comes from the same root as communication. The ability to communicate and dialogue even on the most controversial issue is a concomitant of commitment to *koinonia*. Much as those from the South have been brutalised by the rich and powerful, at home and abroad, our communication should not proceed by bludgeoning and heaping insults on those with whom we may disagree – that does not make for dialogue.

Proclaim Liberty

The concept of *communio-koinonia* raises the question of ethics as the cement of the world community. Today, precisely because we are more conscious of the global village, we need to have done with such ethics as were shaped by Christendom ideology, and push for ecumenical ethics. Such ethics would affirm (i) a just economy founded on morality; (ii) the immorality of currency speculation and manipulation as a manifestation of gambling; (iii) the undesirability of conspicuous consumption as weakening moral fibre. Since, in our global village, the consequences of the debt crisis do not distinguish between Christian and Muslim, Buddhist and Hindu, we must also seek to address the issue of debt, not just ecumenically, but also through inter-faith dialogue.

4. Preferential option for the poor as a criterion of good causes

I have not here chosen to discuss the economy from the perspective of the rich and powerful. That is for the simple fact that the majority of people are victims of the economic systems of our nations. So while earlier I was pleading for the good life to be measured by what is human, permit me to refine it further. If we put the spotlight on human beings, the centre of that light must fall most intensely on the poor, the excluded, and the marginalised.

Crudely put, the issue is whether our endeavour as religious people in confronting the debt issue maintains the established order or enables religious institutions to fulfil their vocation to bring about the renewal and transformation of all creation. It hardly needs stating that the crisis is integrally linked with the market ideology. Our discussion should be a dialogue between our ecumenical ethics and the market ideology, especially its pursuit of profit.[6]

Conclusion

The Fourth Gospel has in its conclusion some sentences which I dare adapt to this occasion: there are many other things on this subject of faith and debt which could be written; if every one of them were to be written down, the world itself could not contain all the books (John 21:25-26).

I have been trying to make just a simple point in this vast area: that the debt issue is an issue of faith and ethics.

Working within an ethical framework on the debt issue also means being mindful and curing ourselves of some of the philosophical assumptions that we have inherited. We need to be mindful of the enlightenment separation of how we think, and how we learn to be – of knowledge from ethics.

Susan George has shown that if we do not have what I have called an ecumenical ethics to guide our life together in this global village, it is not only the case that the poor will suffer more, but that even the rich and affluent part of the global village will head for self-destruction. She demonstrates convincingly the link between the debt crisis, deforestation in the South (a major contributor to global warming), the unstoppable flow of cocaine to northern markets from the South and job losses in the North.[7]

These home truths make the point that the debt crisis is the tip of an iceberg – a global village that has no time for ethical values shoots itself in the foot and heads for mutual self-destruction. The elements of a faith and ethics approach must involve finding relevant ways to: structure our common belief in a common Creator/Creditor God; implement a model in which what is human is the measure of what is good; build a community of communities; and never lose sight of God's preferential option for the poor.

1. Rene Padilla, The Relevance of Jubilee in Today's World in *Mission Studies* XII, 1 & 2, 1996, pp 12-31.
2. Nicolai Berdyaev, *Origins of Russian Communism*, London: Centenary Press, 1937, pp 225-6.
3. D. Bonhoeffer, *Letters and Papers from Prison*, London: SCM, 1967, p 118.
4. Peter Selby, *Grace and Mortgage. The Language of Faith and the Debt of the World*, London: Darton, Longman and Todd, 1997, pp 73-4.
5. John S. Pobee, Theology in the Context of Globalisation, *Ministerial Formation* 79, October 1997, pp 18-26. Reprinted in *Voices from the Third World* XX, December 2, 1997, pp 69-80.
6. John S. Pobee, *The Worship of the Free market and the Death of the Poor*, Uppsala: Life and Peace Institute, 1993.
7. Susan A. George, *A Fate Worse than Debt: the world financial crisis and the poo*, New York: Grove Weidenfeld, 1988; Susan George, *The Debt Boomerang: how Third World debt harms us all*, London: Pluto Press, 1992; Susan George and Fabrizio Sabelli, *Faith and Credit. the World Bank's secular empire*, London: Penguin, 1994.

Proclaim Liberty

Faith issues and the debt debate:
one person's journey

The Right Reverend Dr Peter Selby, Bishop of Worcester

In this piece, Peter Selby, author of 'Grace and Mortgage: the language of faith and the debt of the world', * explores here how his personal encounter of writing about debt led him to discover the power that money has in the world today. He reflects upon the increasing divinisation of money in today's society, and the challenge this poses to faith.

* London: Darton, Longman and Todd, 1997

It was a faith question that pushed me into the debt debate, and a faith issue that has come out of it. The question I was asking, 'Who is Jesus Christ for us today?' led me to look at where the points of oppression were in today's world. As I looked at the burden of debt facing many of the world's poorest countries I could see it was all of a piece with the explosion of debt in our own.

But seeing that was not enough: I also had the task of writing down what I saw. That process communicated to me something of the sheer weight of debt and its effect on the lives of people. It was a weight I found I was feeling in my own hands as I tapped the keyboard of my word processor and in my reluctance to get up in the morning for another day's writing. For debt is indeed a weight which communicates itself even to the observer, and we know as we look at the problem facing the world's poorest countries that, for far too many, it is a weight beyond lifting.

That calls for reflection but above all for action; those of us who gather at the Lambeth Conference this summer of 1998 with the concerns of the Anglican Communion on our hearts and minds must give our all to helping to lift this weight and trying to ensure it bears down less heavily on our brothers and sisters.

The economics may be complex; but the end result we are seeking is not hard to describe: a world where all nations can participate in the world's sufficiency. But as I thought about these things I was very aware that I did so as a person from the North of the world, the one-third that consumes more than it needs. It was not enough to be aware of the poor in our midst, those who face in our own societies a burden very similar to that which is borne by the poorest nations. Christians from other parts of the world visiting our country so often speak in amazement of the poverty they find here, and wonder how it can be that such a situation could exist in the presence of such wealth. What is it that allows that to happen? And what difference could the justice and love of Jesus Christ make to such a situation?

Proclaim Liberty

To understand the faith issues which lie behind the debt crisis means attending not merely to the burdens of the poor but to what has happened within the affluent world of wealthy countries, and indeed among some of the power elites that rule in some very poor nations too. For the level of debt grew to crisis point because in the early 1970s, a process began which vastly increased the quantity of money in circulation in the world. And as the amount of money in circulation exploded, so did the speed with which it could circulate, helped by the technological brilliance of computer networks world-wide.

As a result, money has increased dramatically in its power. This is not a statement about wicked or greedy people, though of course the explosion in the quantity of money has made it something strongly desired and that has produced the inevitable harvest of greed and over-indulgence. But more serious in its effect is the simple truth that quantity means power, and the power comes from the fact that the world has seemed to depend more and more on keeping the process of monetary expansion going. The value of money depends essentially on people retaining confidence in it; and their confidence depends on it fulfilling its promise to keep growing.

So politicians world-wide have felt driven to take whatever decisions were needed to sustain public confidence in money. In one sense this is not new: in making decisions politicians have always had to think about the financial cost of those decisions. What is new is that they have now had to pay heed to the needs of the monetary system itself, constantly acting to maintain its value and strength. This is simply because money has become something we feel required to believe in and to sustain. An increasing amount of attention is being paid to money as an end in itself, and often at huge human cost.

Money has always required faith. Once you stop bartering and use the instrument of money, that instrument needs trust. In the history of the world many different things have been used as money: shells, silver, other metal coins, paper notes, and most recently numbers on a screen.

But they have one thing in common: money only works while people trust it to, and nobody can trust it to work if they do not believe others will continue to trust it to do so. So we support each other's trust in money so that money can continue to work. But at some point (I believe we have come to that point and indeed passed it), the faith we place in money becomes something more than the trust we put in the instruments of our everyday life (that our cooker will work or our car get us to our destination), or the trust we rightly place in our fellow human beings, and becomes more like the trust which I believe belongs to God alone.

Increasingly I see the citizens of the world's more affluent countries come to believe in money as the only adequate security in life and the only proper measure of the value of persons and ideas. This is not necessarily what they want to believe: most people when you ask them will still identify with the biblical text, the love of money is the root of all evil. They may even misquote it as the idea that money itself is the root of all evil, and profess to believe that many things in life are more important than money, and to try to live their lives on that basis.

Yet everywhere the signs are that the power and quantity of money is changing our behaviour, and that our beliefs are conforming to the behaviour that seems to be expected. The language of accounting, or investment and profit, encroaches on ever greater areas of our lives. More and more, the signs are that money comes to be seen as the saviour from a dangerous future, and as the judge between courses of action in the present.

Saviour and Judge. Are not these the attributes of Jesus Christ, and only of him? Is not what we see a process that can only be called the divinisation of money? And in that situation it is hardly surprising that the poor, those most excluded from what money seems to be able to buy, assume that in the acquisition of money lies their only hope. It is a belief that bears fruit in gambling and crime, the poor person's only route to the riches which seem in turn to be the only route to happiness.

Proclaim Liberty

We shall not, in any future I can foresee at the moment, live without the benefits that money undoubtedly confers in enabling the easier exchange of goods and services. But we can and must notice what is happening to us in the affluent world, and challenge the false faith that confers divine powers of salvation and judgement on a mere human invention, however useful it might have been in human history.

My recent experience is that in naming this issue I have found an echo in the consciousness of many Christians who have not previously allowed it to come to the surface of their minds or been encouraged to voice their concern; but once the subject is named they find much to reflect on and a new dimension to their discipleship.

So I bring to the Lambeth discussion this summer more than a concern to discover with others what we as Anglican Christians can do to relieve the poorest nations of the terrible affliction of debt. I hope we shall be able to look at it as a major issue surrounding the lifestyle of the better off as well, who have come to think that credit and debt are the normal, if not the only, ways to live. This may mean individuals, communities and nations having to look at ways to base their economies more on thrift and self-sufficiency and less on the practice of spending today what we hope to have tomorrow.

But above all this, I hope we shall be led, as I have been, through an examination of the crisis of indebtedness to a deeper understanding of what it means to believe in a God who has promised to give us sufficient for our needs, who has placed us in the midst of a rich and sufficient creation which is intended to be here not just for us but as the bearer of God's praise for all eternity, and as an inheritance cherished for our children and grandchildren. I hope we can learn in a fresh way, through a penitent examination of what reliance on credit and debt has done to the poorest of the earth, what it means to trust in a Saviour who came to free us all from the abject life of debt-slaves into God's children's glorious liberty.

I hope, that is to say, that it can be clear that what we are about in seeking remission for the world's poorest nations is a way of representing among us, in the money-language we are all so good at speaking and understanding, the grace of a God who has created a world to be ruled by means of mercy rather than fear, generosity rather than meanness. This God is known already among many of the poorest better than among the wealthy. What we need most of all for this task is a renewal of our faith more than of our economics.

My own journey of thought in this matter began with a question of faith and continued as a journey of discovery about the tyranny of debt which binds so much of the world, rich and poor. Now it has led me on to a question which sounds from the heart of the Gospel: is it true that the world was made by an act of grace, saved by a costly act of mercy and can now therefore live in the power of that grace? And if it is true, can that truth be represented and lived out where, in the current world, it will mean most and witness most clearly, in the way we apportion and regulate the money-wealth of the world?

I believe the answer appears in the heart of the Gospel too: the Lord's fateful last days were inaugurated in the cleansing of the temple, the opening of the house of prayer to all nations, and the removal of that most excluding of barriers that human beings can construct against others, the barrier of money.

There will be a great deal of debate among us this summer, and rightly so, about the best means to alleviate the debt of the poorest nations. I believe that below the surface it will also be a debate about the faith of us all. If in this matter, one that is apparently about economics, we can discover a faith, even as little as a mustard seed, that under God we can discover new ways of living and trading together, then that faith will indeed grow to encompass the whole of our living. For once we have been redeemed from acting towards one another as creditor and debtor, we shall find that in all spheres of life there is a more excellent way of being together, as sisters and brothers.

What then must we do?

The Right Reverend Laurie Green,
Bishop of Bradwell

This piece is from Laurie Green's booklet, 'Jesus and the Jubilee: the Kingdom of God and our new millennium.' * In this extract, which follows on from his analysis of the jubilee message in both its Old and New Testament contexts, he looks at the relationship between Jesus' context and our own, and at how we are called to respond to the international debt crisis. Debt, he suggests, is a structural sin which calls for repentance on the part of the wealthy. Acting to bring about its cancellation is a first step in working towards the Kingdom that Jesus proclaimed.

* Urban Theology Unit, Sheffield, 1997. Reprinted with permission. Full text is available from the UTU, £1.50.

Proclaim Liberty

The Kingdom is both experience and hope – experience of forgiveness, of transforming love and of the presence and power of the Holy Spirit, hope of fulfilment in the midst of the frustrations, fragmentations and ambiguities of history, in the midst of suffering and death.

While we walk with this experience and this hope, we are called to provoke temporary and partial jubilees, moments of justice, here and there, in the Church and in society. Even if the world is resistant and the Church frequently opaque, we must not let the dream go stale. Because when we dream, it is God who dreams in us. Our mission is to inaugurate new ways, new experiments, new signs of the coming Kingdom. And we are called to start with ourselves and with the Church, adventuring in new styles of life, new gestures, new beginnings (Opiyo, 1996:35). [1]

So writes Aloys Opiyo in an article in which he spells out why he sees a relationship between the Kingdom Jubilee that Jesus proclaimed, and our own confrontation with the international debt of the poor countries as the third millennium approaches.

It is certainly clear from the recorded teaching of Jesus that he did not expect his followers to be passive in the fight against sin and debt but to engage both with its symptoms and its causes, in ourselves, one another and in our society. In the Lord's Prayer, for example, he teaches us to say: 'Forgive us our debts, as we forgive our debtors' (Matthew 6:12, King James Version). Likewise, in Matthew 25:31-46, Jesus tells the parable of the sheep and the goats, thereby making it evident that we are to be judged according to our response to the generosity of God in his being in the world in the lives of the hungry, the thirsty, the homeless alien, the naked, the ill, and the prisoner.

In response to the Christ event we are now expected to play our part in the jubilee way of life, and seek to transform the world of sin through enacting passionate signs of the Kingdom. Our engagement with the powerful structures of sin and debt in the world will be the authenticating signs of our own salvation. As committed Christians there is now simply no way that we can allow ourselves or our Churches to await the Kingdom's consummation in idleness, destructive consumerism and social irresponsibility, but by caring behaviour and responsible stewardship (Opiyo, 1996:35).

The early Christian Church sought to rise to this challenge and we read in Acts 4:34 that:

> *there was never a needy person among them, because those who had property in land or houses would sell it, bring the proceeds of the sale, and lay them at the feet of the apostles, to be distributed to any who were in need.*

We may feel that the Church today has failed to follow this early example and is more like the older brother in the parable of the Prodigal Son, who was more concerned with his own well-being and inheritance than with freedom and release for his brother (Luke 15:11ff).

But the Church is called to be the privileged instrument of the Kingdom, participating in the breaking in upon history of the liberating will of God. We should therefore be in the forefront of every call to see sin and debt released from those who are down-trodden by it, and in our age we have a striking example of just such a need that we cannot remain silent.

As the twentieth century draws to a close we are confronted by one of the most heinous assaults on the poor ever known in history, and from which each citizen of the rich countries of the world significantly benefits to the detriment of the poor. It is a new form of slavery or bondage, which was initiated when very cheap and substantial loans were cultivated among poor developing countries by the owners of petro-dollars. This surplus petro-dollar capital derived from the super-abundance of oil in the world market, and rich bankers became keen to find any opportunity of reinvestment of these surplus moneys, even at comparatively low rates of interest. However, with the world oil crisis of 1982, these petro-dollars dried up, whereupon the debtors saw their future dry up too as the financial conditions under which they had incurred the loans changed radically in favour of the rich creditors.

According to World Bank figures, this indebtedness by the poor to the rich world now stands at more than $2,000 billion, and despite all their attempts to repay such heavy loans, they are finding the task impossible. The debts are still rising because, among other things, changes in currency values are manipulated to the advantage of the rich countries so that, although the poor countries produce more today than in past years, they receive less additional income for their exertions.

It is indeed a form of slavery. In 1995, for example, the developing countries were due to pay $1 billion more to the International Monetary Fund than they were due to receive from it, even though such a transfer of wealth to the rich contravenes the IMF's purposes.

The rich countries through the IMF and the World Bank, together with their influential control of the Paris and London Clubs, are aware that it is not in their own financial interest to squeeze the poor of the world until they suffocate and so they themselves are beginning to speak of restructuring the debts so that the immediate burden is lifted a little.

How very alike this is to the situation in Jesus' time. In the first century CE, poor Palestinian peasants were increasingly dependent upon loans to pay their taxes to Rome and their tithes to the temple. Yet, such loans were not readily available. As the Jubilee Release Year, established in Leviticus 25, approached every 50 years, when all debts were to be written off, no money lender would give credit knowing that the debt would automatically be cancelled within a year or so.

In this context, the famous Pharisee, the Rabbi Hillel, attempted to introduce a sliding scale system which he called the *Prosbul*, to bypass the requirements of the Law of the Jubilee Release Year for lending purposes. This however offered only short-term relief in exchange for long-term penury, and extinguished any merciful light at the end of the tunnel for the debtor.

Proclaim Liberty

Just as then, so the IMF's proposal to re-finance old loans with new loans now merely pushes the poor into a no-hope, long-term commitment to be enslaved to a debt that they know they can never pay.

There is much argument now as to whether the debts were incurred by the present generation of the poor or were wished upon them by previous regimes. This debate is not unlike that which raged at Jesus' time as to whether the sins of one generation should be visited upon the next. When, as recorded in John 9:2, Jesus meets a man who had been blind from birth, the question with which he was confronted was: Rabbi, why was this man born blind? Who sinned, this man or his parents? Jesus counters by saying that it simply is not the point to argue about fault. The glory is that he is to be healed, and the debt of sin, to whomsoever it belongs, is to be forgiven. From being cut off from the wider community by sin and debt, he is healed and liberated into his future so that he himself can be the subject of his own history and not merely the object of another's credit.

So it is with the debt crisis, that as the debate about who is responsible for the debts rages, the grave need for remission escalates. In Africa, for example, spending on health care is just a quarter of that now spent on debt repayment, with the budget for AIDS education, clean drains, lavatories and water pushed into subservience to the priority of servicing the debt to the rich world.

The way in which the rich world manages the debt, meanwhile, is itself a grotesque replay of the way in which the priests and Pharisees of first century Palestine used debt to keep their peasants subservient and quietened. If a poor country asks for help or remission, it is visited and advised by the world's rich bankers, through the Bretton Woods institutions, and made to reorganise its economic strategies internally and externally. Only if it abides by these stringent monetarists conditions is it given assistance, but the price is very high. Usually it is demanded that it cuts back on expenditure on vital services such as education and health and devalues its currency, which in turn increases the costs of imported medicines and food.

When rich countries offer loans they naturally incline towards assisting countries that are stable, but this often means that dictatorships are preferred to democracies which, by definition, must be less stable due to electoral changeability of government. The United Kingdom has lent more to Nigeria than any other country and General Abacha, its dictator, is known now to owe it more than $2.2 billion.

In addition to a preference for dictatorships, the rich countries usually tie their loans, so that only specified goods can be purchased with the money, usually of course to be spent in the country from which the loan originated. It is interesting to note that for this very reason, no less than 96% of debt owed to Great Britain by the poorest countries of the world is owed to the Export Credit Guarantee Department![2] It has also been noted that the goods which the credited countries are expected to purchase with the loans are often at substantially higher cost than would otherwise be available on the open international market.

It is this slavery to international debt which stands head and shoulders above other forms of contemporary oppression and which comes most obviously to mind when we compare today's issues with the theological and ideological engagement of Jesus in his day. International debt is crying out for justice, and above all, release.

There are, of course, many other examples of structural sin evident today but I suspect that by engaging in this most obvious of strangleholds on the world's poor we will in turn be taught to become more sensitive to other forms of oppression both at home and abroad. Engagement with this issue will raise our social awareness of the nature of our corporate sinfulness and bring us that *metanoia* repentance of which Christ spoke repeatedly. We will become more aware of the burden of debt shouldered by the poor of our own land, by the squalor in which many are expected to live and bring up their families, by the alienation and fragmentation in our own society. Above all, we will become more aware of the underlying debt of sin that upholds these conditions. Once that repentance is forthcoming it then becomes much more possible to seek out the causes and act accordingly. This is Kingdom awareness and Kingdom Release action.

As we approach the millennium celebrations, one such action for which Christians and other people of goodwill are together pressing is a remission of the international debt owed by the poor to the rich countries of the world. This would indeed be a fitting jubilee to celebrate 2,000 years of our era.

It is exciting to feel that there is a possibility that the voice of the world's poor may be heard as the twentieth century draws to an end, and although we may find it difficult to accept, in return for these initiatives the poor countries of the world will bestow upon us many gifts and privileges. First, they will give us who are rich a new realisation of the truth about ourselves and the basis of our wealth. This is the first stage on the road to the *metanoia*, or repentance, that Jesus called us to.

Second, they may well forgive us as we release their debts. So a two-way mutuality of release will occur. Third, they will renew our vision of the world as a place where simplicity, solidarity and compassion can have pride of place. And finally, as the parable of the sheep and the goats promises, they will help us see God in the poor.

1. Aloys Opiyo, Jubilee: a model for mission, in *The Millennium Jubilee*, CAFOD, 1996.
2. The Export Credit Gurantee Department (ECGD) is a government agency which provides insurance to UK companies who do business in risky markets. When a deal goes bad, the ECGD pays off the UK company and takes on responsibility for the debt.

Proclaim Liberty

Afterword
Jubilee 2000: a debt-free start for a billion people

Ann Pettifor

Ann Pettifor, the director of Jubilee 2000* in the UK, explains here how the campaign began and what it stands for. She makes clear that confronting double standards in international financial relations, and ending the injustice at the heart of the relationship between creditor and debtor nations are Jubilee 2000's main goals. Finally she outlines the main demands of Jubilee 2000's petition.

* For more information write to Nick Buxton, Jubilee 2000 Coalition, PO Box 100, London SE1 7RT.

Jubilee 2000 began as the vision of one of the descendants of a British anti-slavery campaigner: Martin Dent. In 1996 he persuaded a group of us to turn his idea into reality. With the support of Christian Aid, CAFOD and Tear Fund, we started the campaign in a shed on the roof of Christian Aid's building in Waterloo – with only the promise of money, no supporters and one member of staff.

Within two years Jubilee 2000 had become an international movement of ordinary people, objecting strongly to a global financial system that leads effectively to debt bondage; and bringing real pressure to bear on leaders of the world's most powerful economies. In that sense we reflect the movement against slavery in the 19th century. That too was an international movement, led by resistance from slaves in the South, and supported by ordinary people in the North that objected to their governments' role in the slave trade.

What does Jubilee 2000 stand for? Above all we challenge the injustice inherent in international financial relations. We assert strongly the co-responsibility of creditors as well as debtors for the creation of high levels of debt. We go further: we assert that the powerful have more responsibility, because of their leverage over the international financial system. We recognise equally that elites in debtor countries have an in-built incentive to over-borrow. Invariably they are in political office for periods much shorter than the full repayment term of a loan. However we seek to highlight the lack of discipline in the international lending process, which encourages reckless lending.

When we first raised these objections, our voices were heard only in the wilderness. The 1997 Asian financial crisis changed all that. Now there is widespread recognition that Asia's crisis was precipitated by reckless lending – and by the insistence of western governments, through the International Monetary Fund (IMF), that capital markets be forced open and deregulated.

Proclaim Liberty

At the time of writing (Spring 1998), the Asian debt crisis is still being played out. Private bankers that lent money without consideration for the capacity to repay, have been bailed out by the IMF, backed by taxpayers in rich countries. At the same time the people of Thailand, Indonesia and South Korea have been 'buried in debt', to quote the *International Herald Tribune*. A new debt crisis is in the making.

The lack of discipline in international lending can largely be blamed on the absence of fair, legal supervision of international financial relations – to the absence of an international bankruptcy law. When Pan American recently went bust, its Directors immediately filed 'for protection from creditors'. When sovereign governments run out of reserves of foreign currency with which to pay foreign debts – both private as well as government debts – they cannot 'file for protection'. Instead private debts, as in South Korea and Thailand, are effectively nationalised, and the government brought under intense pressure to divert resources from other spending to repay creditors. The pressure is applied by OECD (Organisation for Economic Cooperation and Development) governments, through the IMF. The IMF is both a major creditor in its own right, but also the agent of all creditors – private and public. There is no international, independent 'receiver' to offer protection to debtors, and to draw a line under debts. There is no objective assessment made of the debtors' ability to pay, and of the losses to be suffered by creditors.

In the case of the poorest countries this situation was somewhat ameliorated in 1996, when the IMF and World Bank decided, for the first time in their history, that some debts of the some of the poorest countries had to be cancelled. They launched the Heavily Indebted Poor Countries (HIPC) Initiative to much fanfare. Under HIPC, an assessment has to be made of a country's ability to pay. Unfortunately this assessment is effectively made by creditors – and as a result of this fundamental flaw debt relief has been minimal.

We note that in past debt relief arrangements for western governments, generous relief was offered, in contrast to what is on the table today through HIPC. Britain and Germany received substantial debt relief after the Second World War – relief which gave their children and grandchildren a future. Germany was not required to divert more than 5% of income from exports into debt service. Today Britain and Germany insist that Mozambique, recovering from civil war and the ravages of apartheid, should divert 20% of her pitiful income from the export of prawns and cashew nuts, to servicing debt.

We reject this injustice and these double standards. It is the fundamental injustice in relationships between debtors and creditors that Jubilee 2000 seeks to highlight. We note for example the contrast in the treatment by creditors of a big bankrupt European company – Eurotunnel – and their treatment of the poorest countries of the world. Because of the protection offered to Eurotunnel by the legal concept of limited liability, the children of the employees of Eurotunnel are protected from being held liable for the debts. British law protects them from suffering as a result of the mistakes of Eurotunnel's management. Not so the children of Tanzania. When the former president, Julius Nyerere, asks: 'Shall we starve our children to pay our debts?' international creditors effectively answer, 'Yes, you shall urgently divert money from health, education, sanitation and clean water – and use it for repaying foreign creditors. And so yes, you must make your children pay.'

The injustice can be illuminated in another way. In Britain a rich businessman, Robert Maxwell, was lent a great deal of money by respectable High Street banks. After his death, they discovered that his company was effectively bankrupt. His sons were challenged in the courts by creditors and others who lost money. The judges ruled the sons were not responsible for the sins of the father.

Contrast the case of bankrupt President Mobutu of Zaire. He shared many of the characteristics of Robert Maxwell. These weaknesses did not

90

deter international creditors, notably the IMF, the World Bank, and the British and American governments. Together they lent him $8.5 billion between 1981 and 1990. This was particularly misguided because in 1980 the IMF had asked a respectable German banker – Erwin Blumenthal – to investigate the Bank of Zaire. He reported to the IMF's managing director that it was utterly corrupt and rotten, that no creditor could ever expect to get their money back. The following year the IMF granted the Bank of Zaire the biggest loan ever given to an African government.

Now the reason for this was not just incompetence. The Cold War was still being fought out in that region of Africa, and Zaire was a convenient buffer against the threat of communism in Angola. But whereas the sins of the Maxwell father were not visited on his sons, the sins of Mobutu and his supporters are being visited on the sons and daughters of Zaire. Today the poor people of the new Democratic Republic of the Congo are diverting precious resources that could be used for economic recovery and rebuilding into the coffers of those who backed Mobutu.

So first and foremost Jubilee 2000 challenges this injustice, these double standards in international financial relations.

We note also that high level of debt in developing countries is used as the mechanism for ensuring intervention by western governments (through the IMF) in the running of those economies. The IMF dominates every attempt by debtor countries to seek debt relief. No country may come before the Paris Club of creditors seeking to reschedule her debts, without first jumping economic hurdles set by the IMF, and adopting an IMF structural adjustment programme (SAP) based on a set of policies defined as 'the Washington Consensus'. These policies are used to force poor countries to open up their markets to western traders. In contrast the IMF does not bring pressure to bear on western governments to open up their markets to traders from the South who wish to sell textiles, lemons or wine into western markets. The European Common

Proclaim Liberty

Market erects strong barriers against such traders. In the United States, farm subsidies and trade barriers protect strong vested interests. It is not possible for poor countries to sell rice into the markets of Japan.

We reject these double standards for rich and poor countries.

Furthermore, we have considerable doubts as to the effectiveness of economic policies imposed on indebted nations by Western creditors. We note that the chief economist of the World Bank, Joseph Stiglitz, in a speech in Helsinki, Finland, on January 7, 1998, attacked IMF economic conditionality as 'the dogma of liberalisation [which] has become an end in itself and not a means to a better financial system.' He argued that 'the set of policies which underlay the Washington Consensus are neither necessary nor sufficient, either for macro-stability or longer-term development.' They are 'sometimes misguided' and 'neglect fundamental issues.' We agree. He argues that these policies have not been imposed on highly indebted countries like the United States. He notes that 'had this advice been followed (in the United States) the remarkable expansion of the United States economy would have been thwarted.' Yet these policies are effectively imposed on sovereign developing country governments with high levels of debt.

We reject this injustice and these double standards. Our demands are spelled out in the Jubilee 2000 Petition. This has quickly become a global petition, a form of global graffiti, with people all over the world putting their stamp on it – through thumb prints, signatures and other forms of personal identification. By 1998 it was being signed in over 60 countries.

The Petition is carefully worded.

First we call for the cancellation of 'unpayable' debts – ie not all debts. If a debtor country has debts of $10 billion and can only afford to repay $1 billion we call for the write-off of that portion of the debt that is not payable. The key of course is in defining that which is payable.

We call for debt relief to be given to the most impoverished countries, not all developing countries.

We call for resources freed up by debt relief to be directed to the poor. There is a common misunderstanding that Jubilee 2000 is calling for debtors to be given additional resources through debt relief. This leads to concern that corrupt elites will benefit. Debt relief on its own will not necessarily result in additional resources – it will only remove a burden. Many countries need additional resources – in which case they need both debt relief and more aid in the form of grants. We believe that Africa, for example, needs both debt relief and a Marshall Plan of aid if her peoples are to recover from the deep depression of the 1980s. If there are additional resources made available, we insist that conditions are placed on governments to ensure these resources are diverted to the poor.

We lay great store by transparency – both in the lending process, but also in agreements for debt relief. We want the people of indebted countries to be made fully aware of any relief being granted to their governments, particularly if additional resources are freed up by the process. We want ordinary people in creditor countries to be made aware of how and why their governments make loans to the poorest countries.

Finally we take as our deadline the new millennium. We do this to put pressure on creditors, and on ourselves to build up the momentum of the campaign. But above all, so that millions of people in developing countries will be given a real reason to celebrate in the year 2000.